TEACHING MUSIC APPRECIATION THROUGH LISTENING SKILL TRAINING

Teaching Music Appreciation Through Listening Skill Training

EDRIE THOMAS

Parker Publishing Company, Inc.　　　　West Nyack, N.Y.

© 1972 By

PARKER PUBLISHING COMPANY, INC.

West Nyack, N.Y.

Library of Congress
Catalog Card Number: 72-181391

Printed in the United States of America
ISBN 0-13-892653-0
B&P

To My Father

John Phillips Thomas

How To Use This Book

This book presents a method, containing detailed procedures, for training of individual listening skills. It is extended to a degree where a student becomes capable of gaining the composer's complete communication in a music work through the hearing sense alone.

The "how" of teaching music appreciation has always fallen far behind that of teaching performance. Most teachers have felt uncertain and frustrated in attempts to teach it effectively, because they are aware that young adult years are the ideal time for such instruction. This is because the emotions are begining to mature and deepen, and because much of music literature was created for listeners with at least a measure of maturity.

This book has been written for teachers to share the positive and effective answers so badly needed for so long. The method presented has been used for a decade with teen-agers and adults. Its effectiveness has been established and it is pleasant and deeply satisfying to use.

The author's search for a method of developing listening skill was instigated by two observations repeatedly made in the class-room. The first was that secondary school students and adults came to general music and music appreciation classes with skill adequate for listening understanding of folk music, "popular music," and music of stage and films. When they listened to these kinds of music in class, students worked effortlessly. At the same time students gave evidence that they regarded the class as "easy credit" for repeating what they already knew how to do.

The second observation was that when these same students were presented with the more complex and unknown music works such as intricate jazz and Modern, Romantic, and Classical Period music, they generally found the music beyond comprehension. They could not hear a melody or separate one sound from another.

The situation caused frustration for the teacher. Student needs were not being met. Outcomes failed to meet the expectation of school administrators and curriculum designers who hoped for instruction which would give students continuing aesthetic satisfaction from listening to enduring works of music.

Experiments were started to find what added skill had to be developed in listeners to make them capable of hearing and recognizing the sounds of music elements in much more complex pieces. The answers which eventually evolved are the basis for the method presented.

Material is presented in concise segments, describing procedures for an activity. They resemble a segment from a teacher's lesson plan. One of these can be read in a few minutes and put into action at once. Each is designed as a specific step in achieving the objectives.

The teacher using this method realizes, very early, new feelings of self assurance and achievement in his work. The objectives are crystal clear and the tools are effective. Unbelievable as it may appear, the students become motivating agents for fellow students who are not yet in the class. Frequently non-class members drop in to look around the music room and to express their anticipation for future enrollment. Those who have completed the course come back to tell the instructor how they miss music and to express wishes that they might have continued longer in advanced courses.

The overall way in which this method differs from conventional methods is that it deals squarely with the truth that music communication takes place only through one's direct hearing, and his awareness of his reaction to the sounds he hears. The training steps, geared for the average student ability level, compel him to become involved, then carry him forward in graduated steps which he can achieve with success. He has opportunity to establish hearing identity of each element individually, and then to gradually identify each from other elements sounded with it. As training progresses, the needed hearing exposure time constantly diminishes. He is not placed in a position where he is over-challenged and thus caused to cease trying.

Many students who return years after taking the course, or who are encountered at concerts, comment that music is a different subject because understanding and appreciation increase as the years pass. This, too, is revealing.

The method was developed on the premise that music communicates feeling and perception through the reaction of one's hearing senses to sounds. Each music element, such as melody, calls up its own separate reaction in the listener. The extent to which the listener can hear any one of the elements well enough to become aware of his reaction to it determines the success of the communication. When an individual is judged highly sensitive to music rhythm, for instance, it simply means that he is instantly and keenly aware of his feeling and perceptive reaction to rhythm sounds.

Since music sounds are of fleeting duration, the more capable listener is the one who acquires instant reaction awareness of an individual element. The listener who can react with awareness to each of several elements sounding in combination becomes skillful, and receives the entire communication inherent in the music sounds.

In most of the training activities, short excerpts rather than entire compositions were chosen to pinpoint the hearing attention on the sounds of one music element at a time. As an example, an excerpt in which the theme sounds are clearly etched against background effects readily brings perceptive and feeling reaction awareness to a listener who is trying to identify the theme. An individual's concentration span for intense listening is generally short in early training experiences. The excerpt stopped short of exceeding that span.

Class membership for listening skill training is best restricted to twenty-five or less. These students require more individual attention and encouragement from the instructor than is necessary for performing students. Experiments with larger groups have repeatedly demonstrated that desired results diminish in direct relation to increase in the size of a group.

It became obvious early in experiments of the method that music already familiar to the trainees was undesirable for use in the exercises, except in those for tone color, because majority of listeners would revert to former careless, widely-divided attention habits. The new habits of keen attention must be well established before the former ones can be eliminated.

The instructor may find it preferable to make tape recordings of the excerpts rather than risk loss of attention by students while he hunts for the starting place on a disc. This goes well providing the music department has excellent equipment and can maintain a high standard of production. If the recorder is one which is passed around a building from room to room it is very often found to distort music production. When it does it should never be used. Most teachers become adept at locating the starting place on a disc after a little practice. It is well to turn down the volume and place the needle just before the point where the excerpt begins. The volume can be turned up as it is reached.

The term "aural image" in the method refers to the sound image established in individual memory while listening, plus the memory of the individual's perception and feeling reaction experienced during the time he was listening to the music.

Evidence is strong that an aural image, in recall, which is made with sharpness and depth of perceptual and emotional reaction, is apt to become indelibly established. This fact has significant connotations for the listening instructor in choosing recordings and equipment.

"Reaction awareness" refers to the experience of being exposed to sounds sufficiently long and deep that one reacts in his feeling and perception to those sounds and recognizes his own reaction.

Edrie Thomas

Acknowledgments

The following persons have my deep and lasting gratitude for the help they gave me in writing this book:

My sister, Arvilla T. Wells, who typed the first manuscript, and who always found time out of a busy schedule to give help, moral support and encouragement.

My niece and nephew Gloria T. and A. Glenn Foster for their enthusiastic and constant, critical help during the writing of the manuscript.

Mabel L. Brooner who typed the revisions and the final manuscript. She was always cheerfully available and efficient.

The countless music listening trainees who gave their trust and cooperation to me during the series of experiments which led to creation of the method.

Contents

13

TEACHING MUSIC APPRECIATION THROUGH LISTENING SKILL TRAINING

CHAPTER ONE

Developing Strategies for Initiating Hearing Reaction Awareness

This book provides the music appreciation instructor with explicit directions for leading listening-skill trainees to achievement on four successive levels of ability. They are basic for music appreciation development:

First: trainees learn to identify, through the hearing sense, individual sounds of melody, of rhythm, of tone color and texture, and of harmony.

Second: they become aware of the separate feeling and perceptive reactions which are activated by the sounds of each music element.

Third: they continue to reduce the required time for the first two steps to happen. Music sounds are of such short duration that the response to them must become instantaneous.

Fourth: they learn to accomplish the above steps with several music elements sounding at the same time.

These skills bring trainees to readiness for receiving the direct and full communication contained in a composer's music. The ability to understand communication in music is customarily called music appreciation.

N.B.: *Excerpts from music works were chosen for use in exercises when they presented one music element obviously standing out from other sounds so that listeners could identify it positively. Where only one excerpt is given, it is intended as a sample. It is one which has proved effective with a wide variety of listening trainees. The teacher may choose other music if he prefers as long as it meets the same requirements.*

There has been no attempt made to include samples of all varieties of music in the examples. The sole concern has been to suggest examples suitable for needs of the training procedures, and to lead students to develop advanced listening skills.

Examples from contemporary composers' music are taken mostly from their less complex works. Their advanced works have very few examples of the kind of excerpts needed for training exercises. The advanced music of these composers comes in for its long-merited attention as the listening skills are established.

The exercises designed to develop hearing of music elements are most effective when presented for short periods of time. They demand mentally alert response to a degree which cannot be sustained long without fatigue. Experiments have demonstrated that changing to an exercise for a different element revives an alert response.

Include exercises for three different elements together with singing activity in each class period. Give six to twelve minutes on any one element. Add a few minutes of listening to a whole selection on the level of student understanding. Change the order of presentation each day to retain interest. Do not, at any time, give a continuous series of exercises to completion of one objective.

As the listening trainee succeeds with these exercises, he passes through an extended evolution. He may have been the type of listener who experienced music in a pleasant, drowsy reverie. He may have habitually attended to the music sounds from the outer fringes of consciousness while his thoughts wandered, or may have become partially preoccupied with other thoughts or views. To the trainee music listening becomes a moving and highly dramatic experience. He seeks to gain the composer's meaning as it was conceived and created in the themes. The listener experiences, in the abstract, the motion, tempo, pulse and vigor of the rhythm. He lives the suspenseful interest and satisfactions in the harmony. The clarity and resonance radiated through musical tone color electrify his mental and emotional response. He is vitally alive and alert, and he is privileged.

The listener must acquire ability to center and sustain attention on his hearing sense before he can cope with the first step. There is evidence that most people are not capable of doing this at will.

In our system of communication and education it has been the practice to repeat things a number of times before an idea dependent on the hearing sense for expression could be heard, understood and retained. Directions or instructions containing more than one or two short statements are usually given in writing in order to establish their content. It has not been our policy to train the hearing sense to respond accurately with only one hearing. The visual sense has been given broad and extended training; in comparison, training of the hearing sense has been neglected.

The first exercise, which follows, has proved effective in leading listeners to gain the required ability described above, and to do it with moderate ease.

AN EXERCISE WHICH COMPELS
INSTANT REACTION AWARENESS

Explain that listening is a mental activity set in motion by alerting the hearing sense and sustaining it as the center of one's attention.

Recall a mental picture of the catcher on a baseball team preparing for action. He assumes an alert physical position, keeps his eye constantly on the pitcher's hand which holds the ball. All other concerns are banished. He remains intent on catching the ball.

Recommend that students take a similar position mentally in order to succeed in the exercise you are about to present.

Mention the very short duration of music sounds. One must be very alert to "catch" them for they come in rapid succession and are very soon gone.

Arrange for them to be ready with materials to write.

The exercise should be given in six to eight-minute spans at least three times per week.

Exercise 1

Tell the class that you are going to dictate a series of five numbers once or at the most twice. Speak at the average speed and not too loud.

Direct them to watch for a signal from you before they write the numbers, because you want them to retain the image of what they hear for a short time before writing it.

At first withhold the signal for a very few seconds. Gradually lengthen the time as they become more experienced.

When you have completed three series of five numbers, write the numbers on the board and ask them to check their answers. If it appears that five are difficult as shown in the answers, do another series of five. On the average five numbers are easily heard and written on first trial.

Exercise 2

Papers from exercise 2 should be exchanged, corrected in class and the marks recorded. This practice motivates students to try their utmost, which is important.

Continue dictating and adding a sixth number, a seventh, and so on until they can do a series of ten with ease.

Teacher A made practice of the exercises a home assignment, after the first week. Students were directed to meet and practice in small groups or enlist the aid of a family member to dictate numbers while they practiced. He told them there would be a test within the following ten days with expectations of all being capable of accuracy from dictation of ten numbers.

He found that they responded to the above method with enthusiasm, regarding it as a game. Many of them wanted to try three or four additional numbers at the end of the test in order to see how far they could go.

Teacher B had reports from students in later weeks, that their work in other classes improved because of increased attention to hearing. They appeared to value and enjoy having a double gain from their efforts to hear and remember.

Students reported to Teacher C that they found retention easier if they grouped the numbers in two's and three's in their thinking as they listened to the numbers.

The number dictation exercise proves to be of great value in gaining powers of concentration in hearing. It establishes realization that hearing and retention are dependent upon a receptive, alert mental condition. Indifference and daydreaming are banished because each individual must take responsibility for response by writing the evidence.

The improved hearing efficiency demonstrated by students after succeeding with the exercises amazes the students themselves.

IDENTIFYING TRUMPET TONE COLOR

Experiments and observations have indicated that tone colors of the brass instrument family were easier for students to identify than those of the other orchestra families. Brass tone colors have been found to require less time for creating reaction awareness in the listeners. It appears that their impact on the hearing nerves is more obvious than those of some other instruments. That is the basis for choosing the trumpet as the first tone color to be presented in the method.

The objective is to develop in the listener immediate and positive identification of trumpet tone color as it differs from that of all other instruments. At the same time try to develop awareness, on the part of the individual listener, that he is experiencing a "feeling reaction" to the sounds of the trumpet.

It is necessary for the ear to be exposed for a time of some duration (approximately 32 to 64 measures, with ideal listening response and environment) in order to allow consciousness of the feeling response to surface in the listener's mind.

It is advantageous to present the tone color playing a familiar melody if available. If not, a melody which has proved to have immediate appeal for most listeners is good.

It cannot be too strongly emphasized that the example used should be a good recording played on sound equipment capable of producing a trumpet tone of true musical beauty. Many listeners have acquired an impression of the brass tones as harsh and blatant. This is probably due to having heard them in a situation where the volume was too loud for the area in which it was confined. Brass players and solo-voiced singers sometimes err when performing in an average-sized room by producing volume suitable for a concert hall. This causes a negative feeling reaction, and creates a desire to escape the experience.

Do not offer the student any information about the trumpet, how it is played, or how it should make one feel. The greatest help an instructor can give at this time is to provide an excellent example of the tone color by playing the music. Words have proved to be of no value beyond this point. The listener will become aware of his tone color reaction as it is evoked in him in class. He cannot gain emotional reaction and awareness of a different degree of excellence by means of a verbal description any more than he could react emotionally to a beautiful sunset seen and described by another. One personal exposure is definitely superior to numerous paragraphs of descriptive words. This will invariably prove to be true when presenting tone color of each of the instruments.

Instrumental solos with piano accompaniment appeared to be the obvious choice for developing listener ability to identify the tone color of any one instrument. They were used in early experiments. It was found, however, that the practice did not prepare students to differentiate between one given tone color and that of several other instruments being heard in the background. Excerpts from music works in which the specific tone color being taught had to be identified from several other sounds were adopted because they helped to achieve the objectives in a much shorter time.

An instructor might choose to present a recording of solo instruments with piano accompaniment at the close of exercises for each tone color, if time permits. Selections with sustained tones are preferable to those with brilliant techniques for deepening reaction awareness of tone color.

Verdi's "Triumphal March" from *Aida*, in instrumental version, has served as a good choice for this exercise.

Exercise 1

Start the music after the fanfare and the hymn of thanksgiving, where the trumpet tone color enters on the melody of the grand march.

Indicate when the trumpet is playing by holding up a poster-sized picture of the instrument. Lower it when the strings take over the melody and raise it once more when the trumpet enters in high range tone, playing a rhythm pattern repeatedly.

The music should be repeated. Before beginning the repeat,

ask the class whether the trumpet is playing two or three notes to a beat on the rhythm pattern. If the students request another repetition in order to check on the rhythm pattern, so much the better. That lengthens the exposure to the tone color.

Establish understanding that the development of instruments was motivated by realization that the tone color of each instrument created a different feeling-reaction-response in the listener. This development expanded the expressive possibilities from which the composer could choose to best communicate his feelings and meanings.

Instigate a short discussion to elicit feeling toward color as it affects the visual sense. Ask how many favor one color or another. Most will have a definite and often strong sensitive awareness of their feelings on the subject. Mention that they will discover this to be true as well in relation to tone colors of musical sounds.

Teachers have been unanimous in their enthusiasm over results gained from this tone color presentation. As the reaction awareness begins to surface it can be observed in facial expressions as well as through listeners' comments. This music of Verdi has a strong appeal for audiences in general.

OBJECTIVES IN SONG TEACHING AS THEY DIFFER FROM THOSE FOR PERFORMING GROUPS

The objective in singing activities for listening trainees is to create, through group singing, an authentic expression of the feelings and thoughts of the song creators, and to help the student identify with them. This experience has contributed to developing deeper understanding of other peoples and has been influential in discovery by the student of his own deeper emotional reactions.

Establish the understanding that a student's achievement in the listening skill training program is in no way measured by his public performance ability. He is enrolled in listening skill training to learn to hear music and to understand and enjoy what is communicated through its sounds. His progress will be judged solely from that standpoint. Singing activity is included because it contributes to understanding.

Singing activities merit from one-third to one-half of the class time in early weeks of training. Later the time should be reduced.

The students will frequently request this later because they are eager to progress in listening once they have gained confidence in their own ability.

Singing will be the only familiar activity during early experiences. All of the others will be strange and somewhat strenuous at first. When listeners continue too long with the new exercises they will feel mentally overwhelmed and exhausted. The singing will serve as a contrast and a refreshing interval.

Teachers who have worked mostly with special music students in performing groups can experience great frustration if they approach the singing activities in listening training groups with expectations that procedures are to be similar. It is important to look at the following realistic assessment of ways in which the two differ:

1. Performance groups include about one hundred members. Listening groups should be about twenty-five members. Even in a performing group, twenty-five singers sound much different from the familiar sound of a large group.
2. Listening groups are frequently made up of members who have had no public performance experience.
3. Members of performing groups have to be self-confident, competitive and aggressive during singing activities. Members of listening groups generally lack these qualities.
4. Performers accept responsibility for conforming to exacting demands. The other group tends to hide its voice sounds behind the other voices.
5. Performers will respond to sharp criticisms and demands with added zest. The others respond by shrinking from attention. They tell the teacher, through their facial expressions, that they are not pretending to be singers.
6. Many listening students come to the class with a poor opinion of their own musical ability, an opinion not improved by hearing reassuring comments. A change comes rapidly, however, through experiences in which their success indicates ability of which they never dreamed.

The following recommendations have evolved from experiences and repeated evaluations of procedures with listening groups:

1. There is an obligation to teach proper breath control in singing. Help should be given to eliminate any individual habits of singing with rigid jaw, throat, tongue, or lips. Improper breathing habits or rigid muscles make singing an unpleasant activity rather than an enjoyable one.

2. Use warming-up exercises for a few minutes at the beginning of the singing period. Let the students sing the vowel sounds in unison on one pitch, sustaining each for two slow beats. If you play a series of chord progressions with them, they will gain reaction awareness of harmony while they are holding one tone during change of chords. Cadence and various progressions may be used. One is to play the major tonic chord in first inversion twice, followed by IV major and IV minor chords, and back to the first chord. Transpose the chord pattern up six or eight keys as you repeat.

3. This class is not an appropriate place to spend time on advancing music reading skills or advanced performance techniques. If we accept the premise that communication of music takes place through awareness of hearing nerve reaction, it follows that any concern with reading the score or visualizing the score while listening will result in interference by the visual sense with reaction awareness of the hearing sense. This introduces a complication which offers no advantage.

4. The approach to singing activity expressed in "we are going to sing some songs" is to be always avoided. Choose each song for its significance in developing understanding of the feelings, customs and experiences of a people. Present each song as one which is of interest because _____ ; then introduce it as a special song and explain why.

5. Teach the melody on whatever level the students demonstrate their ability to be. If they are without reading skill, teach it by rote. Play the melody with them if they need that help and add the accompaniment later. If they have reading ability, make use of it. If they can sing harmony parts, without taking time for drill, encourage them to do so. Sing with them if it seems to make for

progress. (There is one exception to that suggestion. If you have a solo voice with rich resonance, it usually follows that the students drop out from singing and listen to you, thereby subverting your efforts to gain their involvement.

6. Use simple arrangements of the songs. Avoid accompaniments with complexities that will drown out the student voices or compete with them. Investigate song arrangements with accompaniments which are used by vocal teachers with solo students in the early training period. They are often rich in chord structures of the harmony, which enhances the singer's tone without competing with him. They develop reaction awareness of harmony while he is singing.

7. Do not try to perfect a song in one period through extended drill. It is preferable to work at it for a short time during each of three or four periods in order to complete the learning.

8. The instructor must give considerable help to these students, by stimulating thought and imagination, before most of them will respond to the full meaning of the song. Pictures are helpful. Point out situations which are indicated by the words. Compare feelings expressed in the songs with some familiar experience which awakened a similar feeling. Try to help the student live experiences indicated in the song, through imagination.

As an example, let us review some procedures which have developed a good understanding response to the Czechoslovakian song, "Over the Meadows." Help the students to visualize, in imagination, the wide green meadows contrasted with the bright color of flowers in the sunlight, and a gentle breeze waving the grass, cooling their skin and rumpling their hair. Suggest the motion and activity of the young people. They are roaming along, side by side, some of them hand in hand. The rhythm indicates a carefree, sauntering motion. Companionship is enjoyed. There is no urgency in reaching their destinations.

Few students will have known the pleasure of inhaling the scent of freshly-cut hay. You will have to compensate by comparing it with other pleasant and familiar aromas.

Point out that twilight is coming on. The air cools.

They will not readily imagine the sparkle and rush of a crystal stream down its course from the mountain heights. Show a picture. Describe the vigor and power with which it splashes against the rocks and sends out its deep roar as it passes.

Ponder some on the words, "singing of life so free." The stream dashes on endlessly. Nothing interferes with its motion. Pictures of snow on the high mountains suggest the source of the stream.

Ask them what the words, "calling to me," mean. Discuss them and lead them to agree on a meaning.

After they have learned the song well you may find that they still cannot express the youthful energy indicated in the rhythm. It is not easy to identify with that feeling after sitting motionless in class for several hours. Have them stroll to the verse rhythm and skip with the chorus rhythm. Have them try the song again and the missing expression will come.

You need to achieve the true expression only once by such extended development. Each time they sing it after that the students will create the expression spontaneously, because they will have lived it in imagination and will have grasped its full meaning.

This song has held a favored place with students. Reaction awareness advances through it. They have been brought to see the scenes, feel the motion of the rhythm, imagine the companionship, the scent of the air, the beauty and sounds of the rushing water. They will have learned to express the jubilance and joy contained in the "Hey," so typical in Czech songs. In all, they will have identified with the Czech boys and girls who have lived with it and loved it.

The aural image of that experience will come back many times in future days and years to refresh and reassure the individual in his mental outlook.

9. To overcome daydreaming and reluctant singing response, call the students up in front, a half-dozen at a time, to sing for the class. They may not do too well the first time. They will grumble, but they will enjoy doing it thereafter. If they were uninvolved before, they will change, because they will know that they are going to

have to "put up the proof" of what they are doing. The same change may be observed with a group of experienced music teachers singing together. After one round of small group performance, even they demonstrate a remarkable improvement.

10. Folk dancing experiences, provided in some schools, are of great value to listening skill training. The music instructor can improvise simplified versions of a country's folk dances in relation to their songs. It is a very rich contribution whenever it is available.

11. Play a recording of the song after it has been learned. A recording performed in the country's folk style with typical folk accompaniment is most desirable.

Teacher A had an excellent and well-deserved reputation as a leader of performing groups. His students, as they are sometimes found to do, had spread an image of him for other students as an "exacting tiger." They did this by tales they told of his demands for perfection.

He was assigned to teach a listening training group. The procedures succeeded well in all but the singing activities. His students were all unacceptable for performing groups. His bafflement increased each day.

He became aware that the students he approached as they were attempting to sing ceased to make any sound at all. He sensed then that they were afraid of him to the extent that they would not try. Upon impulse he went over to the piano and stated in an average voice that he was going to sing the song for them because in that way he could express what it meant to him. He asked that they understand that he was not a solo singer but a chorus singer only. He sang the song in a light voice with sincere expression. When he finished, he asked them to sing it with him, which they did. The gesture changed his relationship with the class. They seemed to feel that if he offered to sing for them in only a moderately good voice, it followed that he would not regard their own moderately good voices with disdain.

Teacher B and several colleagues had chosen Benjamin Godard's, "Florian Song," as a good choice to learn in relation to Bizet's music. Their reasoning was that it had enjoyed a treasured place with generations of French people. Some reports were that the melody was an old folk song which Marie Antoinette sang to her children. A second reason was that its style was representative of the many beautiful carols which make up one group of French folk songs.

Teacher B reported great success with the song when they met to evaluate their efforts. The others had found it not too effective. When this held true at a second evaluation period, it required a serious discussion to find the reason. It developed that the arrangement and accompaniment were the reason. Teacher B had used an accompaniment made of simple rhythm and rich chord progressions.[1]

One mother had reported to Teacher B that her teenaged son had been so enthralled with the song that he came home after learning it and insisted on teaching it to the whole family at the close of dinner.

Teacher C had a long, very successful experience with performing groups. His frustrations after two weeks with a listening group, where he attempted to teach singing, were distressing to hear. By the third month of the quarter he was getting very satisfactory results in expressive singing response. When asked how he created such an improvement he related that he discovered that they were not the same kind of students as those he had had before. The performing groups looked over a new song, without being directed, to discover what its meaning was. They mentally outlined what they would have to communicate to make it meaningful to an audience. The listening group was inclined to just sing along on the words with no concern for meaning.

Following is a description of his presentation of a song which will demonstrate his findings:

The song was "Vieni Sul Mar," (Come Sailing With Me), an Italian folk song.

The music and diction were accurate after one presentation, but there was no hint of the Italian style of expression. They were completely uninvolved emotionally. He tried to impart to them how the Italians sang with such enthusiasm and emotional depth. This resulted in gaining a loud forced-voice quality, but they

---

[1]The arrangement was from *Art Songs for School and Studio, First Year*, edited by Mabel Glenn and Alfred Spouse, Oliver Ditson Co., Sole Representative, Theordore Presser Co., Bryn Mawr, Pennsylvania.

remained emotionally uninvolved. That concluded the singing for the day.

That evening as he thought it over he realized that he had tried to activate them by telling them to be emotional, as if they could turn on emotion at will.

His students had never had experience with boats or been near a body of water where they saw boats. These listeners lived near the mountains, and were ski enthusiasts.

The next day he began questioning them about skiing. He asked them what they were anticipating in thought as they so gleefully prepared to leave for a day of skiing. They described the excitement and moments of anxiety as they took off down the hill, the fun of showing that they could make their way through the possible hazards. They described the crisp, cold air on their faces, and the fun of dodging playful companions.

He asked if they thought of anything else besides the ascent and descent of the hill. Snacks, companionship, beautiful scenes, carefree times as a contrast to daily schedules and snowball fights were mentioned.

He suggested that Italian boys and girls probably anticipated many of the same things when they prepared to go sailing. Sailing also requires skill and offers hazards, excitement and challenges. The novice can easily be upset or knocked into the water. If he isn't alert a friend may easily push him off his craft. He showed poster pictures of the Bay of Naples and of fishing boats leaving Sicily.

They began to identify with the fun-loving aspects which could be present in boating, and gradually began to exhibit some understanding. He then asked them to sing the words as if they were sailing, but not to forfeit musical tone, because Italians were famous for beautiful tone color. His objectives were won.

The extra help required by these students changes the approach to teaching a song, but it is well worth it. The singing activity contributes much making students aware of the emotional and meaningful communication of music.

ORIENTATION TOWARD A COMPOSER'S MUSICAL IDIOM THROUGH SONGS OF HIS PEOPLE

In singing the folk songs and songs which have long held a favorite place through the generations of a people, we broaden and deepen our understanding of that people. The songs give insight into the typical feeling experiences, customs and perceptions of those who created them. Such insight into the people of a composer influences and prepares us in a helpful way to understand the communication he creates in his music. Sometimes his themes are taken from folk songs. Whether this is true or not, we find some characteristics in each composer which reflect the influence of his people's expression.

In the following chapters many excerpts which we use are taken from the music of Bizet and Tschaikowsky. Bizet includes many Spanish rhythms in the *Carmen Suite*. It is relative to sing Spanish folk songs as well as those of his native France. Tschaikowsky writes from his impressions received as a visitor to Italy and contrasts them with Russian-sounding themes. The songs from both countries would relate to the study of his "Capriccio Italien."

There are many songs from which to choose. Following is a list of a few which have related well:

Spanish

The Spanish Gypsies	Spanish Folk Song
Cara Niña	Spanish Folk Song
Andalusia	Spanish Folk Song
The Little Town Across the Bay	Spanish Folk Song

French

Marching Through Lorraine	French Folk Song
I have Lost the "C" on My Clarinet	French Folk Song
March of the Toréadors	by Bizet
Florian Song	by B. Godard

Italian

Vieni Sul Mar	Italian Folk Song
Among the Olive Trees	Italian Folk Song
O Sole Mio	by Eduardo Di Capau
Home to Our Mountains	by Verdi

Russian

Brown Eyes (or Dark Eyes)	Russian Folk Song
On, On, Oh My Soul	Slavic Folk Song
Shining Moon	Russian Folk Song
The Peddler	Russian Folk Song

Introduce some folk songs from each country as you present the music of one of their composers.

Setting Up Instructional Procedures to Develop Listening Skills with Rhythm, Harmony, and Tone Color

A teacher who meets his class fortified with the exercise directions presented in this chapter will have the power to draw response from each student in the group. The exercises will lead the student into involvement with genuine music listening. They eliminate habits of daydreaming and place the student in a situation which compels him to accept responsibility for attentive effort and response. They have proven effective for bringing marked progress in identifying and developing reaction awareness of rhythm, theme, tone color and harmony.

PHYSICAL RESPONSE AND PANTOMIME TO AMPLIFY RHYTHM AWARENESS

Exercises should be used for seven to ten minutes, twice each week. The skillful listener comes to sense ryhthm motion, energy output, and speed in the abstract. Physical involvement with rhythm response serves as a basis for that future goal.

Exercise 1

Play a recording of music in 2/4 meter such as Schubert's "Marche Militaire," or one of Sousa's marches in 2/4 meter and assign pairs of students to join hands and walk to the rhythm. Where space permits, the entire class may take part at one time. Where it does not, three or four pairs at a time must suffice, but every class member should have this experience.

Exercise 2

As soon as all are efficient at Ex. 1, repeat the action, requiring them to move exactly together on the beat without joining hands. When the guidance provided by hand pressure is eliminated, attention to the beat must be much keener.

Exercise 3

Repeat the procedures from Exercises 1 and 2 with music in 3/4 meter, selecting music with a pronounced accent such as "Skater's Waltz," by Waldteufel. Direct them to take one step for each measure, and do not permit them to settle body weight on the foot each time it touches the floor. Buoyancy is indicated.

Exercise 4

Play a recording of music such as the Italian, "Finiculi Finicula"·or the Sicilian hunter's song, "Among the Olive Trees," with their accordian style accompaniment, and direct students to join hands and skip in pairs, responding to the beat with accuracy. Insist that feet leave the floor on the hop part of the skip. This will eliminate sluggish foot dragging and make them feel the animation and energy expressed in the music.

Exercise 5

When all are able to do Ex. 4 satisfactorily, have them repeat the exercise, moving as partners without joining hands.

Exercise 6

Play a recording of the "Toréadors' Song," from Bizet's *Carmen Suite* and ask the class to play the cymbals in pantomine gestures, with the recording, as follows:

1. Students are to assume a firm stance, and keep feet apart.
2. Left hand, palm open, to be held above and forward from left shoulder.
3. Right hand, palm open, even with and forward from right hip.
4. Swing left hand down and right hand up with energy, so

that they pass close to each other halfway (no clap).

5. The left hand continues down to a level with and forward from left hip.
6. The right hand continues up to a position above and forward from right shoulder. With dramatic sweep, they will pantomime the cymbals soundlessly at the time they hear the clash in the music. The hands then remain poised in the No. 6 position, ready for the next clash.

Insist on dramatic, energetic gestures. After two or three trials, on repeated days, they should become precise with the beat. All will certainly have experienced the excitement and fire Bizet created in the rhythm.

Exercise 7

Play a recording of the Italian folk song, "Vieni Sul Mar." Direct the students to assume erect posture, remain seated, feet on the floor, and sway right and left on the primary accent. They are to pantomime the motion they would make to retain balance when the boat rocked widely. Do not accept a mere lean to the right and the left. Insist that they imagine and experience the bodily pull which would be necessary against gravity in a real boat-rocking experience.

Exercise 8

Teach the class to clap the rhythm pattern so often found in Spanish folk music, ♪ ♫ ♫ . The teacher will tap a primary beat on a woodblock, using a wooden mallet head, followed by a light tap with the mallet handle on the second beat.

When they are able to respond with precision, divide the group, requiring half to clap the primary beat and slap the knee on the second beat as the teacher had done with the woodblock. Take care that they mark the primary accent clearly. At the same time, the other half of the group is directed to clap the Spanish rhythm pattern. Call several small groups up in front to do this for the class.

Exercise 9

Seat the students, posture erect, feet on the floor. Direct them to tap another Spanish favorite rhythm, ♪ ♫ ♫ . They are to tap the floor with toes only. Insist upon a clear primary accent with animated motion. It is important that the heels not be used because the suggestion of weight will alter the rhythm expression.

Instructor A, who had an unusual faculty for drawing trustful response and enthusiasm from his students, and was therefore given a generous sprinkling of those with a tendency toward reticence and daydreaming, found that these students made amazing progress in overcoming both tendencies. That result was the more unexpected because they were, for the most part, reluctant to try the activities when first introduced.

Instructor B had too little space in his music room to present exercises one through five as described above. After persistent effort he persuaded the administration to reduce his class membership to twenty-six. He was then able to obtain enough space between chairs to allow the movement of the students without interference. At the same time, he altered the exercises as follows:

Students were directed to use their hands as substitute feet and to walk and skip with them on their desks. He could not substitute for the benefits of moving in pairs, which promotes more exact attention to rhythm in order to relate to the partner, but they did evidence significant feeling awareness of response to rhythm.

Instructor C felt uncomfortable about demonstrating the movements himself, but explained what he wanted them to do and then asked for a couple of volunteers to demonstrate for the class. He worked for a short time with them until they satisfied his requirements and then invited the class to take part. His procedure worked very well. They appeared to be motivated by observing their classmates.

In one way or the other, depending upon the situation and personal preference, these rhythm activities can be of significant help in developing for each student an awareness of his feeling, perceptive and firsthand reaction to the element of ryhthm in simple form. They can draw him into identification with the motion, energy output, animation, sense of order and other qualities which the composer created the rhythm to communicate.

INTRODUCING MUSIC SOUNDS TO REPLACE
NUMBERS IN DICTATION EXERCISES

The following exercises provide the teacher with means for fastening student attention on the rise and fall of sound pitches which make the tone patterns of a theme. Once the student becomes proficient in this, he readily identifies a theme. With a number of varied repetitions he finds a theme easy to retain.

Explain to students that in listening to music with understanding, the hearing must be trained to identify and follow the rise and fall of the melody's tone pattern of fleeting sound. It must be done in a manner similar to that of the eye following the word line in reading the printed page. A teacher may place words on a blackboard or paper and direct the students' eyes by using a pointer. In the use of one's hearing sense with sound, there is not a comparable means to direct the ear. They are, for this reason, being asked to make dashes on paper indicating the rise and fall of the sound pitch as they hear it. This provides the teacher with a definite way to ascertain whether or not students are hearing accurately.

As an example, play or sing the first six tones of one of our favorite national anthems, "America," without words, and indicate them on the blackboard with dashes – – ‾ _ – ‾ .

One can work with the following exercises for about six to eight minutes without straining the attention span. Present a few of them three times a week. After the first day, have them exchange papers and correct them in class. The grades should be recorded in order to motivate students to make the utmost effort. Always play the tone patterns again while they observe corrected papers.

It will be necessary to play patterns several times during the first exercises.

Exercise 1

Sound the following five tones ascending: middle C D E F G, and call attention to the stepwise rise in pitch of each successive tone.

Reverse the direction and call attention to the stepwise drop in pitch of each successive tone.

Place representative dashes on the board and repeat each one.

Exercise 2

After arranging for pencil and paper for students, present the following patterns beginning in the octave between middle C and treble C. Repeat them in the octave above and the octave below. Direct the students to write the representative dashes.

C ↑ E G ↓ E C
C ↑ E F G G
C ↑ F A ↓ F C C

C ↑ E ↓ B ↑ C D ↓ C
C ↑ F A ↓ G E C C
C ↓ G ↑ C E E ↓ D C
C ↓ A F ↑ G A B B C
C ↓ B ↑ C ↓ A G G ↑ A C

Instructor A, who had worked with many special groups, decided at first that Ex. 1 was too easy and was unnecessary. He began with Ex. 2. He reverted to Ex. 1 the next practice period because there were some students who proved unaware of the rise or fall in pitch. Some would lower dashes when the pitch sounds moved up. In nearly every group there are some of these.

The fact is more surprising when it happens in groups where melodies have been sung well. When asked to hear without using their voices, they were confused. Although many will try at first, do not permit them to hum the tone pattern while writing dashes.

Instructor B had available in his school some excellent instrumentalists. He chose the ones with the most musical tone quality in the three string sections, the flutes, English horns, and bassoons and used them to play the tone patterns for his listening classes. His idea was to expose them to tone colors which were less familiar to student ears than piano and brass. He reported that it proved rewarding later in tone color training.

He found, too, that there was an obvious drop in accuracy on the papers of dash patterns as he changed from piano to the other instruments. This was at first attributed to their lack of hearing experience with the less familiar tone colors.

After a few trials he became aware that listeners were very much intrigued with the hand motions, facial expressions and manners of the performers. The visual sense was drawing attention away from the hearing sense. His remedy was to place the performers where they were not in visual range of listeners. Accuracy of dash patterns went up to a marked degree.

Instructor C made it a rule to gradually reduce the number of times he repeated a tone pattern after the first three practice periods, and concluded that it promoted concentration.

The teacher will find the results from tone dictation exercises rewarding. They have been found to show an early improvement in hearing concentration, pitch pattern identification, and last but certainly not least, in self-discipline.

IDENTIFYING TRUMPET TONE COLOR FROM COMPETING SOUNDS

The exercises are designed to make progress in establishing an aural image of the trumpet tone color. Students have to pay intense attention to it in order to sort its tone color out from the background sound effects which are present in each of the excerpts.

These exercises are best limited to about eight minutes at one time.

Prepare students for writing and direct them to answer with the words ACCOMPANIMENT or MELODY, according to which role they hear the trumpet playing in each exercise.

Exercise 1

Excerpt: opening measures of Tschaikowsky's "Capriccio Italien" through the bugle call and the French horn and trumpet tone color to the end of the drum roll.

Present it with the explanation that it is an excerpt to review trumpet tone color. They will demonstrate how well they identify it by writing their choice of the two words.

Its sustained tone style offers an opportunity for an extended exposure to the tone color and to gain a strong reaction awareness to it.

Play it a second time and more if students need and request it.

Exercise 3

Excerpt: play "Capriccio Italien" about 1/3 inch before the end of the record. Begin where the basses play a bombastic primary accent and the trumpet answers in a triple-tongued pattern.

After the papers are checked and collected, the term "triple-tonguing" may be explained and added to their vocabulary. Play the excerpt once more.

Excercise 3

Excerpt: opening measures of Bizet's "La Garde Montante" from the *Carmen Suite*. Play through the distant and close-up bugle call, on through the two presentations of the theme by the woodwinds—the trumpet doing a sharp textured rhythm and tone pattern in competition.

When the papers are collected ask for a show of hands for each word. All will mention that they heard the trumpet on the bugle call. Call for a volunteer to clap the rhythm pattern played by the trumpet in Excerpt 3. Close by playing a recording of "Light Cavalry Overture " by Von Suppe´.

Teacher A found the listeners impressed by the somber sound of the trumpet tone color in the first part of "Capriccio Italien." They had thought of trumpet tone as being always bright with a "sharp-edged" tone.

Students required a number of repetitions before they could identify the triplet from the following longer note in the triple-tonguing heard at the end of "Capriccio Italien." The teacher had asked them to ascertain whether the sounds were just a series of triplets or if they could hear any additional notes. They insisted on a number of repetitions before they discovered the longer tone which followed each triplet.

This teacher had devised a strategy to get them to hear the tones with much longer exposure and at their request. In such a situation student concentration is much more intense than is acquired by simply asking them to hear it a number of times.

Teacher B had several trumpet players in the class. They were very appreciative of the musical tone color in the opening excerpt of "Capriccio Italien." Their expressions of praise for the constant perfection of tone color throughout the long sustained tones generated awareness and enthusiasm in classmates.

Teacher C's group identified the tone color with fewer trials, and proceeded to develop a knowing comparison of the contrast between trumpet tones and those of other instruments being sounded at the same time.

They judged the effect made in the closing part of "Capriccio Italien" to resemble a bomb-like sound from the basses, and the trumpet sound to resemble sparks flying.

They expressed interest in the contrasts of smooth, high woodwind tones and "sharp-edged" trumpet "chatter" in the Bizet excerpt.

Following the exercises with trumpet tone color in Chapter 1, and those above, students have demonstrated a much greater sensitivity and more rapid reaction awareness to trumpet tone color. They have given evidence of this by volunteering comments about hearing it in other exercises where they were not being asked to give attention to it specifically.

CONTRASTING MAJOR AND MINOR MODES

Most students will have recognized that major mode differs from minor mode somewhat, but few will have given sufficient attention to the modes to have gained reaction awareness of each. These exercises are capable of sharpening the awareness. They also develop recognition of the contrast one mode makes with the other through the composers' employment of them.

Five minute presentations, two or three times weekly, are recommended for the exercise.

Exercise 1

Play a major scale on the piano at medium tempo and repeat it at least twice, directing the listeners to concentrate well so that the aural image of the sounds will be retained.

Exercise 2

Play the I IV V chords in the same major key.

Exercise 3

Play the harmonic minor scale and repeat it several times.

Exercise 4

Play the I IV V chords in the same minor key.

Exercise 5

Play the major scale and follow it at once by the minor scale starting from the same note. Repeat them, after asking the students to detect which tones of the major scale are lowered to make the minor.

Exercise 6

Play the I IV V chords in the major key and follow at once with the I IV V chords in minor.

During the following days play each of the six exercises in the octave from treble C upward and then from bass C upward.

Exercise 7

Begin with middle C and E above on piano and ascend by

consecutive major thirds up to middle G and B. Descend in major thirds.

Exercise 8

Begin with middle C and E^b and ascend by consecutive minor thirds to middle G and B^b.

On other days repeat exercises seven and eight in the octave going up from bass C and from treble C.

When you feel satisfied that they readily recognize reaction awareness of each mode, through hearing, arrange for students to have some paper and pencil to write whether each of the following themes are in major or minor. Be prepared to repeat each example several times.

It is strongly recommended that excerpts be taken from recordings of the authentic version of the music. When the theme is played only on the piano, it alters the composer's expression and to some extent introduces a distorted image because of the substitute tone color.

Exercise 9

Excerpt: the second theme of Bizet's "Gypsy Dance" from *Carmen Suite.* Though it is in E minor, it begins on B↑ E F$^\#$ G A B E ↓ B. It begins on measure 49 of the selection.

Exercise 10

Excerpt: theme one of "The Toreadors" from the same suite by Bizet. It enters in string tone color after a rather lengthy introduction and is, of course, in major.

Exercise 11

Excerpt: first theme of Smetana's "The Moldau," often called the river theme. It first enters about a quarter-inch over on the record band. It enters in violin and oboe tone color, and is in E minor.

Grade the papers in class and permit the class to hear excerpts once more.

Teacher A questioned the class about how they made the identifications of major or minor. After some discussion they came to a conclusion that one judged mostly by the way each made him feel. This was a welcome answer because it gave evidence of reaction awareness.

Teacher B followed the exercises by having a twenty-minute song review with the class, including some in major and some in minor. The class was asked to identify each. Finally he reviewed the Spanish folk song, "Spanish Gypsies." It caused some consternation because the first, second and fifth lines are in minor, while the third and fourth are in major. Most students identified each after a few repetitions.

Teacher C's class entered upon a discussion started by a student's comments about major mode being brighter and happier sounding. This led to many students taking definite sides about which mode they favored. Since the decision is made by individual feeling reaction there was no "right answer." He got them all to agree that the two modes give added interest by the contrast they offer.

These exercises have been found to be very helpful in establishing reaction awareness to major and minor modes, and making secure that source of communication between the composer and the listener.

MAKING EVALUATION OF PROGRESS

Ask students to write responses.

1. Dictate several tone patterns of eight tones each to be represented by writing dash patterns.
2. Prepare and present several eight-measure excerpts in 2/4 and 3/4 meter. Play on piano or have taped excerpts from recordings. Use selections other than those used in exercises, choosing music with a strong primary accent. Ask students to write the signature of the meter they hear.
3. Present at least two excerpts with trumpet tone color and ask students to class the trumpet part as melody or accompaniment.
4. Present several excerpts in major and minor mode, other than those used in excercises and ask students to identify each.

APPROPRIATE SELECTIONS FOR TEST EXCERPTS

Trumpet Tone Color

Haydn's "Concerto For Trumpet."

2/4 and 3/4 meter

Strauss Waltzes
"Dixie"
"Marine Hymn"

Major and Minor

Trio part of Schubert's "Marche Militaire,"
with major first theme and minor second theme.

CHAPTER THREE

Capitalizing on Familiar Experiences with Elements of Music

The aspects of listening understanding presented in this chapter are vaguely familiar to most trainees. Our objective in presenting the exercises is to bring each aspect into a sharp focus of attention, to identify it, and to develop rapid reaction awareness of what it expresses as a part of music communication.

DEVELOPING A CONCEPT OF MUSICAL THEME

The listener who has succeeded with number dictation exercises, and has demonstrated accurate hearing by making dash patterns of sounds has developed readiness to begin forming a conception of theme in music. He has sufficient skill to begin identifying the characteristics which make a theme different from melody fragments, musical motives, and connecting passages which are tone patterns and yet not themes.

For some time to come, music will be presented in which the theme stands out sharply from the background sounds, but it is now time to begin laying the foundation for future experiences in which the listener must be capable of recognizing the theme when it is presented less conspicuously. The theme will then be combined with many more competing sounds.

The first concept to be established is that a theme expresses a complete unit of meaning through musical sound. A writer or speaker may express a succession of words without conveying meaning. Sometimes we encounter a person who tries to tell us his idea by starting but never completing a sentence. We become bewildered. An unfinished sentence is similar to a fragment of a theme. Just as the unfinished sentence is meaningless, so is an incomplete theme.

Point out that a theme is nearly always repeated in a music composition of any length. Composers may create rhythm and tone patterns which are also repeated many times, but will be found to be lacking in a complete meaning which would qualify them as themes. Establish the firm understanding that theme expresses a complete meaning.

Explain that customarily there are two and sometimes three themes in a composition, and the reason why that has come to be. Repetition of a theme deepens and impresses the meaning. There is a quality of human nature which opposes excessive repetition. It is an inevitable human response for us to balk at it. We find it monotonous and seek escape by withdrawing attention. The need for contrast and variety must be satisfied if interest is to be retained.

Continue on to explain that contrast, when employed to excess, destroys all feeling of unity in a work. If there is too little repetition musical meanings never become established well enough to make an impression. There is a demand for balance between repetition and contrast.

Mention that there have been a few composers who have succeeded in creating a theme with qualities which make it sustain interest throughout a composition without contrasting it with a second theme, but they have been rare in music literature.

Mention that themes are often but not always eight measures in length.

It is recommended that the first exercises present music which has been familiar to the listener over the years.

Give the following exercises from five to eight minutes at any one time.

Exercise 1

Do not have the music scores before the students while presenting this and the following exercises.

Selection: "America, the Beautiful."

Tell the class you are going to play the melody on the piano and direct them to give a signal when they hear the completion of a musical statement or theme.

Repeat the procedure with the second theme.

Refrain from any mention of form or design at this time.

Allow whatever time for discussion and repetition which appears to be needed for establishing identification of each theme.

Exercise 2

Repeat the above procedure with each of the following songs:

Shenandoah	Sea Chantey
Camptown Races	by Stephen Foster
My Village	Mexican Folk Song
O Tannenbaum	German Folk Song
Santa Lucia	Neapolitan Folk Song
Kuckuck	Austrian Folk Song
Prayer of	
Thanksgiving	Netherlands Folk Song
The Minstrel	
Boy	Irish Folk Song

Exercise 3

Selection: "Träumerei" by Robert Schumann.

Use procedure similar to those above. Omit the repeat at the end of the theme and go on with the second ending. Play only the melody.

Some discussion and several repetitions will be necessary for them to discover that there is only one theme.

They may be somewhat confused at the slight alteration of theme after the music modulates from F to b flat major, but they will come to recognize that it is the same theme and meaning.

Exercise 4

Selection: "First Movement" of Beethoven's *Fifth Symphony*.

Play the opening section of the music, from a recording, until it has gone through the theme twice. Ask listeners to hear the music again and to signal when the theme ends the first time.

This will require discussion, repetition, and help from the teacher. Some will have previously held the idea that the four-sound motive is the whole theme.

Ask them if the motive expresses a meaning completely, or if they anticipate something more to follow. In discovering where the theme is complete they develop greatly, and the patience and time required for this to happen are well spent. Emphasize once more that a theme must express a complete meaning.

Most of the song themes will be easily recognized by the listeners with but little help. The inclusion of a number of songs has been suggested to develop in the student absolute assurance that theme is obvious to them. Experiments have indicated that they need a number of examples before such assurance develops soundly.

HEARING COMPARISON OF TROMBONE AND TUBA

Recommended time for tone color presentations is 12 minutes, with 5 minutes for discussion.

Listeners will have some impression of the trombone and tuba as the lower-toned brass instruments. The objective in the following exercises is to develop reaction awareness of the tone color of each.

It is good to display a poster size picture of both instruments.

Excerpts from music literature in which the tuba tone color stands out from background sounds are not numerous. It is of great importance for listeners to hear music where its tone color can be clearly recognized.

Exercise 1

Present the "Third Movement" of Gustav Mahler's *Symphony No. 1.*

The theme will be familiar to students as the melody of the old song, "Brother John."

Begin the excerpt where the tuba begins playing the first theme. It enters after the theme has been played through by bass viol, followed by bassoon repeating the theme.

Play the excerpt several times. Ask listeners to form a strong image of its tone color, and to consider how it differs from that of other deep-toned instruments.

Begin at the first of the movement and direct them to compare bass viol, bassoon and tuba tone colors.

Exercise 2

Present Britten's "Young People's Guide to the Orchestra, Variation L."

The tuba is contrasted by the trombones in this music. This sharpens the image by contrast. Make certain that they recognize which is tuba tone color and which is trombone.

For excerpts of tuba tone color to be used in later evaluation exercises, some good ones may be taken from Meyerbeer's "The Torch Dance."

The trombones have potential for melody and a wide variety of background effects. There are excerpts from many music works which fill our needs for developing reaction awareness of trombone tone color.

Exercise 3

Present the "Finale" of Brahm's *C Minor Symphony.*

Start the music where the chorale theme enters in trombone tone color. Play it several times on at least three different days. It will develop a deep reaction awareness and an aural image.

For evaluation exercise excerpts, the following works include good choices:

> "Prelude to Lohengrin," by Wagner
> "Espana Rhapsodie," by Chabrier
> "Tannhauser Overture," by Wagner
> "Fourth Movement" of *Sixth Symphony,* by Tschaikowsky

Exercise 4

Play the closing measures of Ravel's "Bolero."

Explain to listeners that the trombone is the only wind instrument which can play a true glissando.

Repeat the music several times.

Teacher A's class entered into a discussion about the comparative appeal of tuba and trombone brass colors. This was good because it secured exacting attention to each.

Teacher A brought out the fact that tuba was the foundation tone of the whole structure of the bass choir. There was a substantial dignified character to its tone. The bass trombone had somewhat the same characteristic, but there were some differences which they would discover with experience. Students were deeply impressed with the beauty of the trombone tone color as their reaction to it began to surface.

Teacher B invited a student trombone performer to visit his class and give some special observations about the instrument. He was asked to tell what had motivated him to want to play it more than other instruments.

The trombone player mentioned its tone color of great beauty, its wonderful potential for flexible motion in comparison with other low instruments, and its smooth legato tone possibilities. He also mentioned its suitability for playing bright or mellow tones.

The boy was well advanced as a performer and sincerely enthused about his instrument. His feelings projected in his remarks and appeared to influence similar responses in the listeners.

Teacher C's group began a discussion after a student's remark that it must be dull to play tuba because it seldom had a chance to play melody. This called out the observation that it was too heavy-toned and rather clumsy to play many melodies. An appreciation surfaced for its dignified, earthy substantial sounds. Another mentioned that instrumental and choral music which, lacked the deep resonance of the bass tones, were never quite as appealing and satisfying as when those tones were present. They concluded that melody parts were not as important as the balanced variety from tones of various ranges when the whole communication was considered.

Some listeners have problems in differentiating between tone colors of the very deep-toned instruments. It is not of supreme importance that they do. It is desirable that they become aware of their feeling response to each. The composer certainly was in his choice of tone color most suitable for his intended communication. If he chose tuba for a part, it was because it most truly expressed his meaning more than any one of the other bass instruments.

The reaction created by a contra bassoon differs from that awakened by bass trombone, bass viol or tuba. To the greatest extent possible, it is desirable to establish reaction awareness of the tone color of each one.

INTRODUCING ACTIVE AND REST TONES

Tell the students that active tones create a desire, in the feelings of a listener, for the tones which follow them to move in prescribed directions, some up and some down. The listener has no choice about the awakening of this desire. He becomes involved whether he wishes to or not. The desired ways move to rest tones which satisfy the listener and release him from feelings of compulsion.

When the active tones do not move in the desired direction, the listener continues to feel agitated as long as active tones continue. He cannot seem to break his involvement even if he turns his attention to something else. The desire remains in his mind for the pattern he expected.

The teacher may find it helpful to relate the story which has been handed down about Johann Sebastian Bach and the active tone compulsion.

The family dinner had been delayed for some reason. Bach had continued to work at the keyboard while he waited. When his wife called that dinner was finally ready, he broke off playing right then and rushed to the table. The last sounds he had made were active tones. He began to eat with great appreciation, but the active tones were still exerting their influence in his feelings. At last he left the table, returned to the keyboard and vigorously struck the rest chords for which his feelings had been agitating. After that he returned to the dinner table where he could enjoy his dinner in peace.

Continue on to explain that rest tones are opposite to active tones. They are satisfying and pleasing. They are nearly always heard as the closing tone of themes and of compositions.

The effect of active and rest tones in relation to each other is of such importance that the listening trainee must achieve instantaneous sensitivity to them as they contribute to the music communication.

Give six to eight minutes time to these exercises in any one class period.

Exercise 1

Play the following tones C ↑ E G ↓ F D B and stop.

Ask the class if the final tone was a rest or active one. They will readily answer that it sounds unfinished.

Tell them you are going to repeat the pattern and ask them to sing the expected rest tone which their feelings demand. They will sound the C.

Point out that you had stopped on the most active tone in that key and that the tone which they sang was the most restful tone.

Play the example again and add C.

Exercise 2

Establish the listeners feeling of hearing the F major key by playing it's I IV V I chords.

Selection: MacDowell's "To a Wild Rose."

Play the melody only, on the piano, of the first theme. Play through next to the last tone and stop.

Ask the class to sing the expected rest tone to complete the theme.

Repeat the procedure with several other themes.

Exercise 3

Tell the students that the effect of active and rest tones is greatly increased when chords are used in certain progressions.

Establish the listeners feeling of hearing the D major key by playing its I IV V I chords.

Play the following progression on the piano using the same notes in both hands placed one octive apart:

– –	G	F$^{\#}$		– –
F$^{\#}$	E	– –		F$^{\#}$
			Pause	
D	C$^{\#}$	– –	a few	D
			seconds	
A	A	– –		A

Present several similar examples which can be taken from the closing measures of many compositions. Pause before the last chord each time long enough to make students feel the urgent desire to hear the final chord.

Exercise 4

In this exercise the teacher wants the listener to realize what an impressive tool the composer possesses in the employment of rest and active tones.

Explain that the composer may delay movement to the final rest tones for many measures of music. In doing this he increases the listener's concerned mental effort to reach and hear the final rest chords. This effect also deepens the feelings of satisfaction which come with the rest chord as it finally emerges.

Selection: "Andante Cantabile" from *The Fifth Symphony* by Tschaikowsky.

Play a recording of the closing excerpt where the tone pattern is repeated over and over at lower levels in pitch until it finally comes to that long-sought feeling of rest.

Repeat at least twice.

Other examples suitable for using in the evaluation exercises are:

> Smetana's "The Moldau" closing measures.
> Dvorak's "Largo" from the *New World Symphony*, closing measures.

In the evaluation exercise, stop one of the two examples before the final chord to make them identify the active chord.

RHYTHM PATTERNS ASSOCIATED WITH A COUNTRY

The following exercises serve as a source for strengthening reaction awareness of rhythm and for reducing the exposure time required for gaining it.

Insert the exercises into moments of class time where a change of pace is needed.

Allow six or seven minutes at any one time.

Exercise 1

Teach listeners to respond to the Scotch rhythm pattern:

They may clap, pat knees or tap the floor with their toes.

Divide the class in half. Direct one group to clap an even four eighth notes while the other group does the Scotch rhythm. When they achieve accuracy, exchange patterns with each half.

Play a recording of the Scotch folk song, "Comin' Through the Rye," and direct their attention to the Scotch rhythm which is heard in this music.

Add that when this rhythm is heard in music it is usually an indication that it is Scotch music, or that it was influenced by their music.

Exercise 2

Review the exercise from Chapter 2 in which the two Spanish rhythms were presented:

Play a recording of Bizet's "Habañera" from the *Carmen Suite*.

Direct listeners to indicate when they hear the first rhythm by holding up one finger, and when they hear both playing at once to hold up two fingers.

Exercise 3

Teach students to respond to the rhythm pattern often heard in French music:

Direct them to substitute fingers for feet and to "walk" the rhythm on their desks. This is necessary in order for them to feel the double speed or tempo in the first four sounds.

Play Bizet's "Habañera," again and direct them to "walk" the pattern with their fingers each time they hear it.

If they have learned the French folk song, "I Have Lost the C on My Clarinet," draw their attention to this same rhythm which is employed there.

There is an advantage in the Bizet selection and many others to be introduced later, for frequent exposure of student's hearing to the tone color of strings. There is no need to make mention of the tone at this time, but each string tone excerpt develops a little more reaction awareness of string tone color.

There is considerable evidence that it takes a longer time to develop reaction awareness of the string's tone colors than that of the other three families of instruments. Keep in mind upon each presentation that the musical beauty of the string tone is of the utmost importance. Both an aural image and reaction awareness are being formed by what they hear in your music room.

Exercise 4

Teach listeners to respond to the American Indian tom tom rhythm.

Ask them to clap it or to pantomine the playing of the drum. Practice until they can control the impulse to keep increasing the tempo. Insist on the tempo remaining constant.

Play a recording of the Indian folk music, "The Cheyenne War Dance," arranged for orchestra by C. S. Skilton in his *Indian Dances and Suite Primeval.*

Direct them to pay special attention to their reaction to the repeated rhythm pattern. It expresses an unusual feeling of motion with a constant high degree of energy output.

Exercise 5

Teach them to clap or pat the rhythm pattern of syncopation which is so often heard in American music.

Keep it at slow tempo until all are accurate with ease, in their response.

Divide the class in half. Direct one group to tap the even four eighth notes

with their toes while the other half clap or pat the syncopated pattern. When accuracy is soundly established, exchange rhythms between the two groups.

It is advisable to review the above exercise several times. This rhythm is difficult for many students. Increase the tempo gradually.

Play a recording of the old Negro folk song, "L'il Liza Jane," or one of the other Negro songs where the syncopated rhythm stands out clearly and the music is not too fast or complicated.

Experiments have demonstrated that the listeners cannot identify fast and complex syncopation, through hearing, this early in the training period.

Exercise 6

Teach the class to clap or otherwise respond to the Bohemian folk rhythm called the "Furiant,"

Keep the tempo slow for this rhythm is a great challenge.

Divide the class and give each half a turn at the "Furiant" rhythm while the other half pats one beat to a measure. Review for several different periods before you increase the tempo.

Play Anton Dvorak's "Slavonic Dance in G Minor." Ask the students to signal when they hear the "Furiant" rhythm. It suggests great expenditure of energy. They must be helped to recognize and identify with that degree of energy.

This rhythm requires frequent reviews before it can form an aural image in listeners' minds. It is both strange and intricate. If the tempo is speeded up too soon, great confusion develops.

Teacher A made a practice of reviewing these rhythm exercises for short periods, when students appeared fatigued or preoccupied at the opening of class. He reported that they seemed to enjoy the exercises and that they become alert and ready for further involvement with class work as a result of the activity.

Teacher B used the procedure of calling rhythm on one of the up before the class to do rhythm responses.

He used flash cards with the name of each rhythm on one of the cards. He would flash a card and nod to one of the groups, after which he would give the signal to start.

He assigned the more difficult rhythms to the students who had shown strong independence in the former rhythm exercises. He assigned the easier rhythms to those who had been slower to respond with accuracy. The students who were observing those up in front received repeated reviews through identifying with the groups doing the rhythm. This happened without them realizing that they were being drilled with repetitions.

These rhythm exercises bring great strides in developing rhythm reaction awareness. They help to form an aural image of rhythm patterns of different nations.

CHAPTER FOUR

Effecting Direct Composer Communication–
Advancing with Tone Color and
Harmony Hearing

The instructor now approaches an exciting experience. He has been guiding the students in various phases of listening skill which develop readiness for this time. The teacher is going to create the situation for direct communication from composer to listener, and remove himself from the activity.

The listening trainee will identify the theme, respond to the meaning it expresses, and form a fairly clear aural image of the music, entirely independent of any aid or direction.

In relation to each theme some pertinent information is offered, but it is recommended that the teacher refrain from making any comments about how the music should make the listener feel, or about how it has been found to make others feel. Leave the creation of an aural image entirely up to the composer and the listener. After the image is formed some discussion may be instigated.

In each exercise the listener will be concentrating attention on the theme. In all probability he will be gaining measurable reaction awareness of rhythm and tone color at the same time. When students are asked to recall a theme by singing or whistling it on following days, they usually produce the rhythm accurately and will volunteer that it was played by strings, brasses or woodwinds.

In preparation for the activity the teacher will provide:

1. An excellent recorded performance of the chosen excerpt.
2. The name of the composer and his music.
3. A theme tagged with a name or a number by which it will be known in order to differentiate between it and other themes.
4. Elimination of all competitive noises in the environment, and of any visual displays which might divert attention from the hearing sense. (Words on the blackboard or impressive action pictures have diverted listener attention to the extent that a double number of repetitions have been required before theme identification could be established.)
5. Avoidance of any personal mannerisms or movements which might distract listener attention.
6. Materials for writing.

EMPLOYING DASH PATTERN WITH COMPOSER'S THEMES
Present exercises from 15 to 18 minutes at a time.

Exercise 1

Music work: Tschaikowsky's "Capriccio Italien."

Excerpt: theme beginning about one inch over on the record band where the basses are heard playing a repeated pattern ¯ _ ¯ _ . Mention that the composer wrote the music in memory of a pleasant visit he had in Italy in the year 1880. One theme in the work was taken from an Italian folk song. The other themes include some in Russian style of expression and some in Italian style. The musical styles of these two countries make a vivid and interesting contrast.

Inform members of the class that the theme which they are about to hear will have the reference name of Italian Theme No. 1. It is the one taken from a folk song of Italy.

Request a dash pattern be made, if possible, in one hearing.

Play the excerpt through to where the basses intercept and go romping down a descending tone pattern in which rhythm changes are evident.

Repeat if requested.

Exchange papers and check dash patterns.

Play the excerpt once more while they have the checked papers before them.

Record grades.

Exercise 2

Music work: Tschaikowsky's "Capriccio Italien."

Excerpt: begin same as in Exercise 1.

Explain to listeners that you are going to play a longer excerpt of the same theme heard in Exercise 1.

Ask them to listen to discover how many times the complete theme is played.

Start the music at the place used in Exercise 1 and continue playing until the theme has been heard three times.

Ask students to raise their hands when you state the number of times correctly according to their decisions. Ask if they heard it once, twice, three times or four.

On the following day ask for volunteers to sing or whistle the melody as they remember it from the day before.

Ask them to suggest what rhythm motion seems to be indicated by the music. Is it a slow walk, a sauntering one, or a dance?

Discussion often leads to a conclusion that it suggests care-free young people sauntering along together, feeling no urgency to reach their destinations.

Exercise 3

Music work: Tschaikowsky's "Capriccio Italien."

Excerpt: theme beginning about the center of the record band, where the rhythm changes from 6/8 to 4/4 meter. At that point, the basses repeat the following rhythm pattern ♩ ♫ ♫ . The theme enters on the 9th measure after the 4/4 meter begins.

Inform listeners that this theme will be given the reference name of Italian Theme No. 2.

Request a dash pattern and inform students that you would be interested in any other added observations about the music which they might make.

Repeat as requested.

Exchange papers, check, and then record grades.

Call for review volunteers to whistle or sing the theme from memory on following days.

Exercise 4

Music work: Tschaikowsky's "Capriccio Italien."

Excerpt: begin as in Exercise 3 and extend the number of measures to be heard.

Ask listeners to discover how many times Italian theme No. 2 is played.

Start in place of Exercise 3 and play until the theme has been heard twice.

Ask how many heard it once, twice or three times.

Ask for volunteers to sing or whistle it by memory on following days.

Ask the class to identify the rhythm meter. Allow a few minutes to discuss this and other mental observations listeners hopefully will have made about trumpet tone and other elements.

Exercise 5

Music work: Tschaikowsky's "Capriccio Italien."

Excerpt: theme beginning about five-eighths of an inch before the end of the record band. This theme is in rapid 6/8 meter. Immediately before its entrance the strings are heard in several flourishes as they swell the volume, increase the tempo and then ritard. The theme enters in woodwind tone color.

Inform listeners that this theme will be known by the reference name of the tarantella theme. Explain that the tarantella is a vigorous Italian folk dance.

Request a dash pattern. Warn listeners that the tempo will be rapid, which will demand that they think in faster tempo in order to identify the melody.

Repeat as requested.

Call for three volunteer students to write their dash patterns on the blackboard while other students exchange papers.

Make corrections if needed on the dash patterns on the board. Give the class time to check the papers from the examples on the board.

Record grades.

Repeat the theme while they observe dash patterns.

Exercise 6

Music work: Tschaikowsky's "Capriccio Italien."

Excerpt: begin where the tarantella theme enters and play until sounds imitating the bagpipe begin.

Direct listeners to write the letter "T" each time they hear the complete tarantella theme.

They may need help from the instructor on the number of times they hear the theme. They will be certain about hearing it four times, but may not observe that the theme gets started several times and is left incomplete before the "bagpipe" sounds enter.

Direct listeners in tapping toes on the floor to the exact rhythm of the tarantella theme. This brings awareness of the speed and vigor indicated in the tempo.

Play the excerpt once more. Begin with the tarantella theme entrance and play completely through the imitation "bagpipe" section.

Exercise 7

Music work: Tschaikowsky's "Capriccio Italien."

Excerpt: theme beginning near the first of the record band, three measures after the ferocious rolling of the drums which follows the bugle call.

Inform listeners that this theme will be known as the Russian theme.

Ask them to make dash patterns of the theme as they identify it and urge them to get the pattern with one hearing. The theme is in slow tempo and very obvious.

Call for several volunteers to place their dash patterns on the blackboard.

Ask other class members to exchange papers and check from examples on the board, after those examples have been corrected. Generally students will enjoy competing for a chance to write their examples on the board.

Record grades and repeat excerpt.

Exercise 8

Music work: Tschaikowsky's "Capriccio Italien."

Excerpt: begin at the first entrance of the Russian theme as in Exercise 7, and play until that theme has been heard twice.

Ask listeners to indicate whether they heard the theme one, two, or three times.

Ask listeners to try to identify any brass tone colors, other than the trumpet, which may be sounded in the excerpt.

Allow a few minutes for discussion and repeat the excerpt if there are any disagreements on what was heard.

Exercise 9

Evaluation and review.

Write the theme reference names on the blackboard.

Play the Tschaikowsky themes in the following order, after directing listeners to write the name of each theme as they hear it:

> Italian theme 2
> Bugle call
> Tarantella
> Italian theme 1 (in one of the first three presentations)
> Russian theme
> Italian theme 1 (closing measures of record band)

Exchange papers and check.

Record grades.

On the following day, play the entire composition.

Exercise 10

Music work: J. S. Bach's "Jesu, Joy of Man's Desiring." Orchestra.

Excerpt: begin where the brass choir enters on the chorale theme. The work begins with a rapid motion theme. On the ninth measure, a woodwind choir begins the chorale theme. Where it ends there is a short interval in which the rapid theme is heard and then the brass choir enters on the chorale theme.

Explain to the students that Bach wrote the music with two themes being sounded at the same time. One is moving in rapid motion, sounding three tones to each count. The other theme moves in slow sustained tones.

Tell the class that you want them to make a dash pattern of the slow theme. It will be called for future reference the "chorale" theme.

Repeat if requested.

Call for volunteers to write dash patterns on the blackboard, have papers exchanged, checked and grades recorded.

Play the music from the beginning through the chorale theme by woodwinds, and then by brasses. Ask the class to ascertain the number of times the chorale theme was sounded.

Ask listeners to identify families of instruments heard on the chorale theme only.

Exercise 11

Music work: J. S. Bach's "Jesu, Joy of Man's desiring."
Excerpt: first eight measures.

Tell students you want them to hear the rapid motion theme twice and ask them to memorize it well enough to sing or whistle it—without writing dashes.

Repeat if requested.

Teach students to pat the rapid theme rhythm with fingers on desks or knees.

Teach them to pat the theme rhythm of the chorale theme.

Divide the class in half. Assign one group to pat rhythm of the rapid theme while the other half does the rhythm of the slow theme. When students develop accuracy, exchange patterns.

Play the entire compositions.

Exercise 12

Music work: First Movement of Dvorak's *New World Symphony.*

Excerpt: begin about two-fifths of an inch over on the record band where the third theme enters. The first four tones of this third theme are identical with those upon which the word "chariot" is sung in the first phrase of the song, "Swing Low, Sweet Chariot." It enters in flute tone color.

Request that listeners make dash patterns from one hearing. Do not permit them to hum the tones while they are writing.

Repeat, reluctantly, if requested. One needs to cut down exposure time.

Exchange papers, check, and record grades.

Completion of the twelve exercises with the recommended composer themes has been revealed repeatedly as a landmark of progress in developing the individual listener's self-esteem. Evidence of the progress becomes obvious to the instructor through changes in both attitude and response of the student. Expressions reflecting self-doubt and hesitancy to enter music activities will seldom be heard anymore. Students may ask a question or two to be certain that they understand directions, but questions are asked with the expression of one who is confident and ready to take unhesitating responsibility.

Instructors have attributed the student growth in self-esteem to the following reasons:

1. Listeners seemed to regard these exercises as a proving ground of hearing ability. They had long been inclined to doubt their own ability. They will now have proved to themselves that they have such ability.
2. The listeners found the meaning expressed in each theme had significance for them.
3. The individual student identified the theme and gained understanding of its meaning solely through his own ability and effort. He knew now that he could do the same in future experiences with other music of his choice.

INTRODUCING THE FRENCH HORN

French horn tone color does not prove to be as obvious as that of other brass instruments. It has a faculty for blending into other tone colors which makes it more difficult to identify. The two excerpts which are presented in the exercises should be reviewed during several class periods.

Listeners confuse French horn with trombone when heard from recordings. This continues until reaction awareness of each is well established. French horn tone is often judged to be woodwind by early trainees who hear it from a recording.

Mention that the French horn is often called the alto of the brass choir, but that composers frequently choose it to play the melody. Its predecessor was the long hunting horn, whose tone carried for long distances over the fields. It is rarely heard making blatant or harsh sounds.

Display a poster picture of the instrument.

Exercise 1

Music work: "Waltz of the Flowers" from Tschaikowsky's *Nutcracker Suite.*

Excerpt: begin the music on the fifth measure, where the horn tone enters and play the theme several times.

Introduce the music as an example of French horn carrying the melody. The melody will be familiar to most listeners. This is a great help in that it frees the student from having to identify the melody and the tone color both at once.

Exercise 2

Music work: Charles Ives' "Finale" from his *Second Symphony.*

Excerpt: begin the music about one-third inch over on the record band just after the strings are heard in a frisky motion followed by a ritard. Continue to play until the French horn melody ends.

Ives' presentation of French horn tone color is one of the very best for awakening reaction awareness. Its tones as presented are so musically beautiful and sustained.

Repeat the French horn part several times and then let the music play on to the close of the "Finale."

Other music which includes easily identifiable excerpts of French horn tone, which you may want to use in evaluation exercises, are listed below:

> Weber's "Der Freischütz Overture."
> Beethoven's "Third Movement" of *Eroica Symphony.*
> Beethoven's "Scherzo" of *The Fifth Symphony.*
> Mendelssohn's "Overture" from *A Midsummer Night's Dream.*

Teacher A chose several excerpts which contained one or another of the brass instrument tone colors clearly presented. He kept them easily available for short review exercises. At intervals where the class changed from one activity to another, he would play one and ask listeners to identify the brass tone they heard.

He found that this practice developed instantaneous identification of each brass tone color and that it deepened reaction awareness.

Teacher B made a practice of discussing with the class reasons why symphony orchestras customarily included a very small number of brass instruments, perhaps two to five of any one type, while they included as many as sixty stringed instruments.

He stimulated many thoughtful comments and observations about the comparative tone colors and their effect on listeners. He used the discussion to point out the matter of tone color balance in the large musical teams. He made students aware that brass instruments produce great volume, which can erase most other tone colors from the listener's hearing.

Exercises one and two have established a strong reaction awareness to French horn and developed a deep aural image of its tone color in the trainee. For most students, prior to the exercises, an awareness of the French horn color will have been vague or non existent. After the exercises have been completed, students demonstrate their alert recognition by frequent comments and observations about the tone color when it is sounded in their musical experiences. They do this without being questioned which indicates that horn tone color has gained a significance for them.

HEARING IDENTIFICATION OF CADENCE

Give a brief review of active and rest tones. Follow by explaining that there are active and rest chords in each key which exert an influence on the listener similar to the one made by active and rest tones.

Continue the discussion to add that active chords progressing to rest chords appear at the close of most music. The progression of chords which leads to the close or completion is called *cadence*. There are two well-known forms:

1. Plagal cadence which is the name for the chord progression in which the four chord is followed by the one chord of a key. This cadence is found at the close, and on the "Amens" of many hymns. It satisfies the listener and accentuates the key of the music.
2. Complete cadence is one in which the chord pattern of progression often presents a one chord followed by a four, a five-seven, and then a one chord. This progression builds both greater suspense and stronger satisfaction in listener response. As in the plagal cadence, this cadence accentuates the key of the music.

Exercise 1

Play the last three measures of the Christmas song, "Good King Wenceslas," to demonstrate the *plagal cadence*. Repeat the example several times.

Exercise 2

Play the closing measures of "The Battle Hymn of the Republic" with full chordal harmony to demonstrate the *complete cadence*.

Exercise 3

Music work: Bizet's "Habañera" from the *Carmen Suite.*
Excerpt: closing phrase.

Play the music just short of the final note. Repeat once or twice to make all listeners aware of the suspenseful feeling generated in the desire to hear the final sound.

Play the same phrase through to completion and call attention to the effect of the third from the last tone, with the long pause, as it increases suspense. Repeat several times.

Exercise 4

Music work: "Intermezzo" from Bizet's *Carmen Suite.*
Excerpt: closing measures
Follow the same procedure as in Exercise 3.

Exercise 5

Music work: Verdi's "Triumphal March" from *Aida.*
Excerpt: closing measures.
Follow the same procedure as in the two former exercises.

REACTION AWARENESS OF TWO OR MORE MUSIC ELEMENTS AT ONCE

The exercises to follow are strenuous. Use only one in any one music period.

Arrange for writing materials.

The exercises are designed for challenging the listeners to identify and gain reaction awareness of the two elements at once.

Ask listeners to write the meter signature of the music they hear, such as 2/4, 3/4, 6/8. Warn them that there may be some meter changes.

Ask students to write an abbreviation of the theme name each time they hear the theme. If it is played five times the name is to be written five times in abbreviated form.

The Russian theme may be written as R. Th.

The First Italian theme may be written as I. Th. I.

The Second Italian theme may be written as I. Th. II.

The Tarantella theme may be written as T. Th.

Remind listeners that the meter is the steady, basic beat or pulse in the rhythm.

Exercise 1

Music work: Tschaikowsky's "Capriccio Italien."

Excerpt: begin two measures before the first entrance of Italian theme I, where the basses are repeating a pattern ‾ ‿ ‾ ‿ .

Play through to where the 4/4 meter begins and go on for four more measures. As the 4/4 begins the basses are performing a rhythm pattern 𝄴 ♩ ♫♩ ♫♩ .

Ask students to write the meter heard as the music begins and to be certain to write the signature of the new meter if one enters. At the same hearing, listeners are to write the theme name every time they hear a theme completed.

Repeat more than once if requested.

Exchange papers and correct in class.

Repeat the music while students observe the corrected papers.

Exercise 2

Music work: Tschaikowsky's "Capriccio Italien."

Excerpt: begin where the 4/4 meter enters just before the second Italian theme and continue to play until the Russian theme has been completed once. The Russian theme enters where the music changes definitely back into 6/8 meter.

Ask listeners to write the meter signature which begins the excerpt and the signature of any meter changes which come later in the music. They are to record the theme name each time it is heard.

Exercise 3

Music work: Tschaikowsky's "Capriccio Italien."

Excerpt: begin with the 6/8 meter and the Russian theme which occurs immediately after Italian theme II ends. Play until the entrance of the imitation bagpipe sounds.

Ask students to write the meter signature and theme names as in the other exercises.

There will be no change in meter. The tempo will pick up before the tarantella theme approaches. It will be quite a challenge for listeners to identify each repetition of the theme.

Offer special credit if a listener describes changes in the tempo of the rhythm.

Repeat as requested.

Exchange papers and check.

Play once more while they can observe checked papers.

The theme exercises just completed are a stiff challenge, but they have not been overwhelming for listeners at this stage of training.

Teacher A customarily reviews rhythm meters the day before he presented the first of the three exercises. He included 2/4, 3/4, 4/4, and 6/8 meters. Students were asked to make physical response to the primary accent in all meters and to the secondary accent, as well in 4/4 and 6/8 meters.

He stressed repeatedly that the beat or pulse was the heart of the motion, tempo, and all other sounds of rhythm which might be adding complexity.

His students demonstrated a high measure of ability in the exercises.

Teacher B conducted a review of themes for short periods, several days before presenting the above exercises.

He made a practice of calling for volunteers to whistle or sing the themes as he called for them.

He followed the theme review with a question about the rhythm motion. He asked what motion might be indicated by the rhythm.

He reported that some had to have help in recognizing the march rhythm on Italian theme II. They also needed help at the change in tempo when the time came for the tarantella theme to enter. Students required help in discovering the exact spot where the meter changes occurred.

There was no evidence of listener doubt about being capable of doing the exercises. Some demanded many repetitions but they worked at the problem with enthusiasm and self-confidence.

CHAPTER FIVE

Expanding Listener Awareness of Melody, Tone Color and Rhythm

In all four sections of this chapter the teacher will be leading the listener to a deeper, sharper realization of his own emotional response to the sounds of music elements. The activities are a series of steps in exploration and discovery through which the individual learns about music's communication and about himself.

HEARING CHROMATIC, PENTATONIC AND WHOLE TONE SCALE PATTERNS

Listeners often experience some feelings of disorientation during their first concentrated hearings of the chromatic, pentatonic and whole tone scales. The average environment and listening experience have established a familiarity with major and minor modes and developed identification of feeling with them. The disorientation comes partly from the fact that tones in the three scales about to be presented, do not awaken a desire for tonal direction through active and rest tones. Each tone is as important as any other one.

Explain that melodies include chromatic, pentatonic and whole tone patterns for more colorful emotional expression and for creating wider contrasts. Explain that the three scales being introduced are not employed as often or as widely by composers as major and minor scale patterns. Each of the three has individual expressive qualities which enrich and broaden the expressive possibilities in a colorful way. If a listener is familiar with these added scale patterns, he more readily responds to them and to the composer's intended mood.

Refrain from comments about how either scale should make the listener feel. Do not offer any explanation about these scales lacking rest and active tone roles in their effect. Until listeners are much more advanced, the chief objective is to lead them to identify the sounds of each scale and gain reaction awareness of those sounds as they differ from the better known major and minor.

Exercise 1

Explain that each tone in the chromatic scale is one half-step distant from those on either side. When the scale is played on the piano, the pianist plays each successive key, white or black, ascending and descending. There are no skips. This makes a twelve-tone scale.

Play the chromatic scale on the piano upward from middle C to treble C and down again to middle C. Repeat several times.

Play in the octave above and the one below.

Exercise 2

Music work: "Habañera" from Bizet's *Carmen Suite.*

Excerpt: begin where the first theme enters and play it through to the entrance of theme 2.

Before presenting the theme tell listeners that the chromatic scale tones are to be heard in this theme. Repeat it several times.

Exercise 3

Music work: Korsakov's "Song of India" from the opera, *Sadko.*

Play the entire composition.

Write the words "chromatic scale" on the blackboard. Ask the listeners to keep faces turned straight front and to turn their eyes to the words on the board when they hear the sounds from the chromatic scale. Repeat the music at least two times in review on other days.

Exercise 4

Explain that the pentatonic or five-tone scale can be made by playing the major scale with the fourth and seventh tones left out. Add that the scale is included in scale systems all over the world.

Play the pentatonic scale on the piano both ascending and descending in the middle octave. Play in the octave above and the one below.

Exercise 5

Music work: the old Scotch song, "Auld Lang Syne."

Play the melody alone on the piano after explaining that it is created from the pentatonic scale tones. Review on other days.

Exercise 6

Explain that each tone in the whole tone scale is one whole step from those on either side. When the scale is played on the piano the player must strike every other key white or black, ascending and descending.

Play a whole tone pattern beginning on middle C and ending on treble C. Descend on the same pattern and repeat several times.

Play in the octave above and the octave below, repeating several times.

Exercise 7

Music work: Debussy's "Nocturnes: Fêtes."

Excerpt: begin on measure 15, where the theme enters in 'cello and bassoon tone colors and then violin tone colors. It is in 4/4 meter. Play through the theme which is four measures long.

Explain to the listeners that Debussy has employed the tones of the whole tone scale to create this theme. Play the theme and repeat it at least twice. Review on several different days so that students will have sufficient exposure to gain reaction awareness of the whole tone scale sounds.

PRESENTING TONE COLORS OF STRINGS

Our objective in presenting the following exercises is to lead the students to instantaneous identification of the tone colors of violin, viola, 'cello, and bass viol instruments. We will return to strings at a later time to present harp and piano tone colors. While listeners are developing identification of the tone colors they will awaken in each individual listener reaction awareness of those four tone colors.

It is of supreme importance to present excerpts of excellent musical tone. Distorted string tone quality can awaken deeper negative responses from the human hearing sense than almost any other sound. It can erect for the listening instructor insurmountable obstacles. As listeners become advanced they will learn to identify and respond to many effects typical of the string family such as vibrato, pizzicato and many others. In the present chapter we are concerned with creating reaction awareness of the rich singing, buoyant tone colors of each of the four instruments. This step is basic for all future music communication through string tone colors.

The tone colors of string instruments require double or longer time of exposure than other instruments to develop reaction awareness in the average listener. The impact string tone makes on the hearing sense proves to be as subtle as the impact of the brass proves obvious.

Display a poster-size picture of each instrument as you present it.

Exercise 1

Present the violin as the soprano voice of the string choir in the orchestra. Omit any reference to its history, how it is played, or how is should make one feel. Let listeners hear it.

Music work: "Triumphal Marche" from Verdi's *Aida* in instrumental version.

Excerpt: begin playing the music at the end of the introduction where the thanksgiving hymn enters. Play to the end of the selection.

Hold up a poster picture of the violin when it is carrying the melody. Lower it when the trumpet takes the melody.

Exercise 2

Music work: "Hungarian Dance No. 6" by Brahms.

Play the entire composition.

Explain that you want them to listen to the violins with the objective of identifying their tone from all other musical sounds.

It will be well to repeat it several times on succeeding days with the objective restated for the listeners.

Mention that the Brahm's music reflects numerous characteristics of the Hungarian gypsy music. The violin has long been the favorite instrument of these people. Many of them have demonstrated special talent for playing the instrument with great beauty.

You may wish to relate the following true story to demonstrate the above point:

In one of the Eastern European countries the government had passed a law requiring gypsy children to remain in one school community during the school year. They were expected to attend school regularly and be responsible for doing passing work.

This was a frustration unheard of by the gypsy people who had roamed for generations, back and forth across Europe, stopping or moving at will.

The law placed truant officers in an impossible assignment. One understanding law maker who knew of the gypsy love for the violin advised the government to offer to every gypsy boy and girl who attended school and completed the year's work a violin at government expense. So great was their pleasure at the hope of owning this beloved instrument that they gave up the old roaming tradition in order to acquire one.

Repeat the music several times.

If the instructor wishes to verify his own hearing identification of themes, there is a very useful dictionary available.[1]

Refrain from showing the score to listeners either from the blackboard or any other way. They can learn to identify through hearing alone. It is desirable that they do this in preference to using visual interference with direct communication through sound.

Exercise 3

Music work: Second movement of Beethoven's *Symphony No. 6.*

Excerpt: begin at the first of the movement. Theme No. 1 begins on the eleventh count of the first measure which is in 12/8 meter. It ends on the second count of measure 7. It is played by the violin.

---

[1] Harold Barlow and Sam Morganstern, *A Dictionary of Musical Themes* (New York: Crown Publishers, Inc. Thirteenth Edition, 1968).

The theme is rather difficult to identify at the first hearing because the other instruments of the string choir are playing a counter theme with harmony parts in a lower range. The lower theme is thought to suggest the sound of a brook. It has often been called the "brook theme."

Ask students to make a dash pattern of the No. 1 theme being played by the violins. They identify the theme faster in this way. The instructor will gain an advantage in that he has a chance to repeat the theme many times. Listeners demand many repetitions for completion of the dash patterns. While they are doing the pattern, reaction awareness of the violin tone color is established.

Listeners generally gain some reaction awareness of the other string tone colors as well during this exercise.

Exercise 4

Present the viola as the alto or tenor voice of the string choir. Explain that composers often employ the viola tone color in playing the same part as another instrument. It blends well with others. It enriches and enhances the tone color to which it is added.

Music work: "Andante" from Beethoven's *Symphony No. 5*

Excerpt: begin at the opening of the movement where the first theme is heard in viola and 'cello tone colors. Play to the end of the theme.

Repeat several times and review on other days in order to establish reaction awareness of both tone colors and theme.

Exercise 5

Music work: Second movement of Beethoven's *Symphony No. 6.*

Excerpt: begin on measure 33. The music is in 12/8 meter. The third theme of the movement begins with measure 33. It is in viola and bassoon tone colors. Play through measure 38.

Repeat several times and review on other days.

While gaining reaction awareness of the tone colors, the listener is forming an aural image of one of Beethoven's most beloved themes.

Exercise 6

Music work: "Adagio" movement of Beethoven's *Symphony No. 9.*

Excerpt: begin on the last note of the 24th measure where theme 2 enters. The meter changes from common time to 3/4 time on the 25th measure. The theme is played in violin and viola tone colors.

Play the following 18 measures which extend to where the 4/4 meter returns.

Repeat the excerpt a number of times during each of several days. Here again, 'the listeners are forming an aural image of theme while gaining reaction awareness of tone color.

Exercise 7

Present the 'cello as the baritone voice of the string choir in orchestra. Explain that it has often been chosen by composers for solo parts as well as accompanying roles.

Music work: "The Swan" from *Carnival of the Animals* by Saint-Saëns.

Play the entire composition. Play it several times and repeat on successive days.

The 'cello plays the melody.

Exercise 8

Music work: First movement of Schubert's *Symphony No. 8 in B Minor.*

Excerpts: begin the music where the 'cello enters on the second theme G ↓ D ↑ G ↓ F # ↑ G A and play through. It comes about 1/4 inch over on the record band.

Repeat the excerpt several times and review on successive days.

Exercise 9

Present the bass viol as the bass and the foundation of the string choir as well as the whole orchestra.

Music work: Gustav Mahler's third movement of *Symphony No. 1.*

Excerpt: begin at the opening of the music. The theme begins after a short introduction. It is played on the bass viol. Students will be familiar with the theme from hearing it in the presentation of tuba tone color. Repeat several times.

Repeat it on several successive days.

Exercise 10

Music work: First movement of *Schubert's Symphony No. 8 in B Minor.*

Excerpt: begin at the first of the music where listeners will hear 'cellos and bass viols in octaves and on the unaccompanied melody of the introduction.

Play the eight-measure melody several times and review on successive days.

Teacher A made a practice of playing only the first small motive of the Beethoven theme in Exercise 3. He would ask students to write a dash pattern for the motive.

As he prepared to continue with the theme he warned students to pay special attention to the fourth and fifth notes of the motive in the second version which they were about to hear, because those two would be altered. With his help and several hearings they would discover that the altered notes had been lowered a whole tone in the second hearing.

He helped them with the dash pattern of the three grace notes which came before the fifth regular note.

A similar procedure was followed in the third figure of notes where they discovered that the fourth and fifth notes had been raised a whole tone from their position in the first version of the motive.

He found that the remainder of the theme was easily identified in dash patterns by the listeners.

Teacher B reversed the order of presenting the four string instruments. He presented the 'cello, viola, bass viol and then the violin. He felt that the middle and lower tones were more familiar to listeners and easier for them to begin identification with than were the violin tones.

CONTRASTS IN PANTOMIME AND RHYTHM
RESPONSE WITH MARCHES

Listeners may have formed the opinion that all marches express identical communication. Marches are regarded as pieces of music suggestive of repeated, precise motion, sounds of fanfare, exciting emotions. Our objective in the exercises is to lead them to discover the variety of communication in march music by presenting three famous marches in contrast with one another.

The exercises are designed to involve students in responding to the communication that makes each of the three marches different in what they express.

In each exercise the listeners are called upon to place themselves, through imagination, in a different situation and to pantomime a characterization which contrasts clearly with those in the other two marches. As the contrasts become evident in student motion and pantomime, all listeners gain an expanded awareness of communication from the music.

Assign one-half to one-third of the class at a time to take part in the march pantomime, in front of the class, while the remaining members observe and suggest which responses are most convincing and which ones need to be developed further.

Students can progress through these exercises from hesitant and unimaginative response to sincere involvement. As they become contributors in creating the contrasting expressions of the three characters, their self-doubt fades. Attention of the listeners centers more and more on creating the character and less upon the individual self. The results of this experience are almost miraculous, because the students begin these activities with the feeling that they're having fun and they come to recognize and respond to a broad range of feelings in their efforts to create a convincing image of the characters by identifying with the characters' emotions and activities.

Individuals discover the musical expression through imaginative participation in portraying the characters. The exercises require a number of rather short practices of around ten minutes in order to give a convincing response to the music. During that time listeners learn to hear the complete communication of the composers. This comes about both through their thoughtful effort and through repeated exposure to each musical selection.

"The Marine Hymn" is used because boys and men respond spontaneously to acting the role of marching Marines.

It is well to grade listeners on their response to each exercise.

Exercise 1

Music work: "The Marine Hymn," anonymous.
Play a recording of the whole march.
Ask students to listen to the music with the aim of visualizing the posture and motion of a typical marching Marine.
Select the first group to go before the class and ask them to march to the music and to try their utmost to create the image of a Marine marching.

When each group finishes ask the observers to comment on the points which successfully portrayed the Marine characterization. List the points on the blackboard.

Call for observer suggestions for improvement where they found the march response unconvincing. List the comments on the board.

Each exercise will require several reviews on succeeding days. When you review an exercise remind students of the comments and suggestions which were written on the blackboard before they begin participation. This keeps their attention on the objective.

Exercise 2

Music work: "Toréadors' Song" from Bizet's *Carmen Suite.*
Play the entire composition.

Ask listeners to try visualizing, as they listen to the music, the situation, appearance, posture and motion of a bullfighter as he enters the arena before cheering spectators. He is moving to the sounds of the march.

Discuss a little how his role differs from the Marine's. The bullfighter must play his role "by ear" in some respects. He cannot follow a well-planned, well-disciplined pattern that is pre-conceived before he goes into the arena. He may not express the positive force and assurance of the Marine. He must be very flexible and light-footed in motion. The chin line posture of the Marine would differ from that of the toreador.

Follow similar procedures to that of Exercise 1.

Exercise 3

Music work: "Triumphal March" from *Aida,* by Verdi.
Play the entire composition.

Ask students to visualize, while listening, and consider the feelings, carriage and motion of a soldier marching in a victory parade before his home town people.

Tell the class something about the splendor of the march as it is presented in the opera.

Follow a similar procedure to that used in the above exercises.

Teachers have sometimes approached the three preceding exercises with some reluctance, fearing that the attempt at some of the dramatic aspects would introduce discipline problems, or that they would direct the attention away from listening to sounds. Doubts have been overcome during the first experience with the exercises.

The students' awareness of communication has been enlarged. The student hears many repetitions of each selection without any feeling of being drilled and without the subsequent loss of attention. His involvement becomes such that he responds to many facets of the music which he may not have recognized as a motionless listener.

IDENTIFYING THEME IN CHANGING TONE COLOR

The following exercises are presented with the objective of strengthening listeners in rapid and positive theme identification, even when tone color is constantly changing. At the same time identification and reaction awareness of tone colors are further developed.

Exercise 1

Music work: "Simple Gifts" from Aaron Copland's *Appalachian Spring.*

The melody of this music is from an old religious folk hymn of our country, also called "Simple Gifts." Teach students to sing the hymn before presenting the Copland music for listening.

The music begins with the theme played by strings in slow tempo. The clarinet enters next on the theme and plays a more extended part of the melody. Following this there are four variations on the hymn tune.

The first time they hear it students may develop a little confusion in separating the connecting tone bridges, between the variations, from the theme.

The first variation is in oboe tone color. In the second one the trombone plays the melody with the strings coming in on the theme later in the style of a round. In the third variation the trumpet plays the melody while the trombone adds harmony effects in the background. The fourth one is played by the woodwinds.

Explain to the students that there will be a presentation of the theme several times followed by variations with short connecting bridges between.

Ask listeners to write down the name of the individual instrument which plays the theme each time it is repeated. If they cannot be sure of the individual instrument ask them to write the name of the instrument family.

Repeat as requested.

Exchange papers and check.

Record grades.

Exercise 2

Music work: First movement of Beethoven's *Symphony No. 6.*

Excerpt: begin on measure 67, where the second theme enters· in violin tone color. The meter is 2/4. Play through the first beat of measure 93.

Ask students to make a dash pattern of theme while you play the four measures of the music. Repeat as requested.

When the theme is identified by all students, ask them to listen to the excerpt and to write the name of each instrument which plays the theme each time it is repeated.

The tone color series on the theme is as follows:

Violin
2nd Violin
'Cello
'Cello and Bass Viol
Clarinet for 2 measures

at which point the bassoon joins the clarinet, completes the theme, repeats it, and brings the music to a pause.

Expect to repeat the music a number of times as the listeners request it. This exercise is a strong challenge for the average student. Many will not be able to identify the bassoon entrance. They may need the instructor's help in recognizing its tone color.

Exchange papers and check.

Record grades.

Exercise 3

Music work: "Scherzo" from Dvorak's *New World Symphony.*

Excerpt: begin about one-fourth inch over on the record band where the second theme enters in flute and oboe tone colors. It is easy to recognize because it begins the same as the opening theme of "Largo" from the same symphony, or it is the same as the theme of the old familiar song, "Goin' Home." Play until the theme is completed. It is played by 'cello and bassoon.

Students will not need to make a dash pattern of the theme for it is obvious. Repeat twice.

Ask students to hear the music and write the name of the instruments which play the theme.

The tone color series is as follows:

Flute and Oboe
Clarinets in octaves
'Cello and Bassoon

Repeat as requested.
Exchange papers and check.
Record grades.

Motivating Listeners Toward More Subtle Identification of Theme, Rhythm, Tone Color and Key

Instructors presenting activities to follow will find they contribute well to achieving the objective of drawing trainees into a deeper individual commitment of attention to the sounds of music elements. Objectives are aimed at some less obvious aspects of musical expression. The listener must seek them with his hearing sense and attention to a greater degree than he has before.

The listener, in making these commitments, realizes growth of ability and increased assurance of his capacity for listening. He makes substantial progress in understanding the music's communication.

The trainee discovers that he can react with awareness to melody, rhythm and tone color all at once while adding gradual awareness of background sound effects.

ESTABLISHING THE ROLE OF
ACCENTS IN RHYTHM

Explain to the group that accents in music indicate the meter to listeners as the time signature and bar line indicate meter for music readers.

Direct students to regard accent as an energetic thrust forward in motion and time. The thrust may be aimed at an extension of only two beats or perhaps as many as twelve beats.

Add that the thrust is made on the accent and the motion is felt to continue on through all the beats of a measure. When the motion is extended over a long measure it may seem to weaken or fade some. A secondary accent prevents this because it reinforces the energy needed to carry the motion to the measure's end.

Suggest that accents represent stress and the unaccented beats may be regarded as a coasting motion which requires no effort.

Ask trainees to recall the mental picture of an ice skater who makes an energetic thrust forward on one foot and coasts for some distance with no additional effort.

Mention that in a Strauss waltz the dancers' only energetic motion, from an observer's point of view, is made on the primary accent of the music measure. The second and third beat motion give an impression that the dancers are defying the law of gravity. There appears to be complete freedom from effort. This accounts for the general feeling of relaxation which a Strauss listener experiences if he is identifying with the rhythm motion.

In the longer measures such as six-eight, twelve-eight and others, the energy from a primary accent needs renewing. It is customary to sound secondary accents halfway through the measures.

Arrange for writing materials.

Tell the listeners you want them to determine the number of beats they hear in each measure of the excerpts, starting on a primary accent and reaching to the next primary accent. They are to write the number they hear in each exercise.

Exercise 1

Music work: "Skaters Waltz" by Waldteufel.

Excerpt: recorded version of the first 16 measures with their repetition. It is in 3/4 meter.

Direct students to write a mark of number 1 for each primary accent they hear and to write at the end the number of beats, accented and unaccented, which they heard in each of the measures.

Repeat as requested.

Exchange papers, check and record grades.

Repeat the excerpt and ask them to imagine themselves in motion to the rhythm while they are hearing the music. They may have moved to this music in overt physical response during an earlier exercise. Recall this to their attention and play the music.

Exercise 2

Music work: "Artists Life" by Strauss.

Excerpt: begin the music at the close of the introduction, about one fourth inch over on the record band. A definite 3/4 waltz meter enters at that point. Play through 16 measures.

Follow a similar procedure to that used in Exercise 1.

Finally, play the music from Exercises one and two in contrast to each other.

Ask listeners to decide if there would be a difference in the motion suggested by the rhythm of each waltz.

After considering for one or two hearings, most of them become aware that the Waldteufel music suggests a smooth gliding motion while the Strauss music suggests a motion of light steps on the second and third counts of the measure.

Exercise 3

Music work: "Theme and Variations" on *Pop Goes the Weasel* by Lucien Cailliet.

Excerpt: the first two variations. Start the music where the brief introduction ends.

Inform students that if they hear both primary and secondary accents, they are to make a mark 1 for each primary accent and a mark 2 for each secondary accent.

The measures where Cailliet omits the primary accent and replaces it with a surprise rest, catch some listeners off guard. They write the accent mark down and become the objects of good natured ridicule from fellow students.

Variation one is in 6/8 meter and variation two in 3/4 meter. These two meters can be confused with each other until listeners learn to detect the secondary accents. It helps make students recognize the difference by contrasting the two.

Repeat as requested.

Exchange papers, check and record grades.

Repeat the music once more while they have the checked papers before them.

Exercise 4

Music work: "Cheyenne War Dance," an Indian folk dance from *Suite Primeval* by Charles Skilton.

Play the entire composition.

Instruct students to mark the accents in writing as they did on the other exercises.

Customarily after a few measures have been heard, some listeners' facial expressions reflect doubt. It is well to stop the music and allow time for a short discussion about their uncertainty.

They will have discerned that there is not the usual difference between accented and unaccented beats. All four beats are energetic even though the first one is loudest. The customary coasting feeling on unaccented beats is missing. They become aware, too, that the heavy beats create a different feeling reaction.

Play the music after discussion and let students mark the accents in writing.

Repeat as requested.

Exchange papers, check and record grades.

Play the music once more.

Exercise 5

Music work: First movement of Mozart's *Jupiter Symphony.*

Excerpt: begin on the first entrance of the third theme, about one-half inch over on the record band. It comes in string tone color and in common time. Play through the theme.

In the first section, known as the exposition, there are five divisions. The first one ends in a ritard followed by a sustained tone. The second, third and fourth divisions each end on a pause rest. Just beyond there the strings play a descending pattern and then theme three enters. Play through the theme several times before asking students to write marks.

Inform listeners that the theme begins just after the second beat of the measure. Ask them to mark both primary and secondary accents.

This third theme is in a style very characteristic of Mozart. It is a favorite with every listening group.

Repeat as requested.

Exchange papers, check and record grades.

Play the music once more as papers are observed.

Exercise 6

Music works: both excerpts from Exercises 4 and 5.

Tell students you are going to play the Indian music and the Mozart theme for them to make comparisons. Both have four beats to a measure. Their communication through rhythm accents differs widely.

All groups observe that the Cheyenne music taxes listeners by its indicated physical motion with such great expenditure of energy, while the Mozart taxes one by its demands for flexible mental activity. The war dance suggests relentless, overpowering energy output. Mozart packs complex communication into a few short measures. The latter is both intricate and subtle for the listener. The Indian music is exciting and more obvious.

Take time to discuss and establish a conception of the differences.

Exercise 7

Music work: "Danse Bohème" (Gypsy Dance) from Bizet's *Carmen Suite.*

Excerpt: start the music at the end of its brief introduction. Theme one enters there in 3/4 meter and in flute tone color. Play through the theme.

Ask students to write marks for primary accents and then play the theme. Expect to repeat the excerpt a number of times.

When they have finished ask them to listen again to find if they detect any accents in addition to the primary ones.

They are well able to detect that the groups of sixteenth notes in the second measure on beats two and three begin with a slight accent.

Exchange papers, check and record grades.

Repeat the theme several times.

Exercise 8

Music work: Second movement of Beethoven's *Symphony No. 6.*

Excerpt: accompanying motive, which is often referred to as the "brook theme," at the very start of the music. It is in string tone color. You will remember that there is a higher range theme playing at the same time. Ask them to pay attention to the lower tones. Play three measures. It is in 12/8 meter.

Direct trainees to write the usual marks for primary and secondary accents and to write "G" where they hear group accents in addition to those other two accents.

It rarely requires more than one repetition for listeners to discover that there is a secondary accent on the 7th count, and that there are group accents on the 4th and 10th beats of each measure.

Exchange papers, check and record grades.

Repeat the music.

Exercise 9

Music work: "Scherzo" (Humor) from William Grant Still's *Afro-American Symphony.*

Play the entire short movement.

Write the words "syncopated rhythm" on the blackboard. Ask students to face straight front and to turn only their eyes toward the words on the board when they hear the accent come after the beat.

Repeat the exercise on at least two other days. It is often difficult for trainees to identify syncopation by hearing music at this tempo.

Students like the music and enjoy hearing it over and over. It will prepare them for hearing even more complex works in the same rhythm.

Teacher A found that listeners could readily imagine and identify with the motion suggested by rhythm sounds in the "Skaters Waltz," but the motion of the Strauss rhythm was foreign to their experience. They could not visualize taking a vigorous step followed by two light steps in one continuous impulse.

He asked them to substitute fingers for feet and to "dance" on their desks or knees. He directed them to make a vigorous, short leap to the right on the primary accent. This was to be followed by two light running steps extending the initial motion of the leap. On the following measure the pattern was repeated toward the left. While the demonstration did not imitate the authentic steps of the waltz, their unbroken motion did suggest the extended pulse of motion customary for each measure. It succeeded in giving students the light-footed, weightless feeling characteristic of the second and third beats.

Teacher B asked listeners to compare the tempos of the Indian music and Mozart's music. It often took some time and discussion to establish realization that the tempos were quite similar. Students had judged the Indian tempo to be faster.

He brought attention to the urgency or stress in each of all four beats in the Indian music, even though the first beat had the greatest stress. This led listeners to realize they had mistaken the excitement generated by the repeated stress for a more rapid tempo.

Through continued discussion he developed recognition that the stressed beats of the Indian music brought feelings of urgency and force. At the same speed or tempo the Mozart music stimulated feelings of freedom and animation. This was due to primary accents being followed by a coasting motion, with a re-charge through the lighter secondary accents.

Further discussion and comparison brought recognition that elements in the Indian music were obvious in their expression. All listeners could gain its communication in one or two hearings, even without deep concentration. The Mozart sounds, if heard with a similar concentration, flashed by the listener and were gone before they could be heard and awaken a reaction.

Trainees reached a conclusion that one had to "reach out" mentally to gain Mozart communication even after several hearings. The listener had to make a greater investment of mental effort to achieve a full understanding. At this stage of listening skill development, students appeared to accept the fact as a challenge which was intriguing.

DISCOVERING BACKGROUND EFFECTS IN MUSIC COMMUNICATION

Explain to the class that composers employ background sounds to enhance and expand their communication. The listener who gains it must respond with perception and reaction awareness of these sounds. Each is created to contribute something to the expression, and they must be regarded as significant.

Exercise 1

Music work: "Capriccio Italien" by Tschaikowsky.
Excerpt: begin the music just over an inch from the first of the

record band, where the first Italian theme is heard for the second time. Play through the second and third renditions of the theme.

Ask trainees to listen with special attention for any sounds which are played in the background as the theme is being heard.

Listeners soon discover a ripple of ascending tones from strings and woodwinds. Some students have described the sounds as resembling the action of bubbles as they rise in carbonated drinks or in a glass of champagne.

Exercise 2

Music work: "Capriccio Italien" by Tschaikowsky.

Excerpt: begin the music where the meter changes from 6/8 to 4/4 shortly before the second Italian theme enters.

Mention to trainees that you want them to listen especially for the low range rhythm pattern and that after you stop the music, you want them to pat the pattern on their knees with accents made accurately.

The pattern is 4/4 ♩ ♫♩ ♩ ♫♩ .

It comes out that one hand does the primary accent and the other hand does the secondary if hands are used alternately.

Repeat the excerpt several times after they identify the rhythm pattern and demonstrate it.

Exercise 3

Music work: "Toréador Song" from *Carmen Suite* by Bizet.

Excerpt: begin the music where theme one enters in string tone color at the end of the introduction.

Ask the class to listen for and be ready to describe any sounds other than the strings on the theme.

Students will soon discover the staccato tones by the trumpets which repeat the same pitch on every beat.

Bring listeners to recognize that the sharp-edged, repeated tone serves to keep feelings of excitement at a high level during the melody by the strings. The light, fluent sounds of the strings alone could sound dull and too subdued for the mood without the re-charging sounds from the trumpet. This is true because the sounds of the preceding introduction are so bright and dramatic.

Write the word *percussion* on the blackboard. Direct trainees to keep faces turned straight forward, but to turn eyes toward the word on the board as soon as they hear percussion sounds replace those of the trumpet with a sound on each beat. This happens after the theme has been played twice.

Exercise 4

Music work: "Toréadors Song" from *Carmen Suite* by Bizet.
Excerpt: the opening 16 measures.

Direct trainees to listen for the pattern being played in the background by the basses and to make a dash pattern of the tones. The pattern is: ⁻ _ ⁻ _ ⁻-_ .

Repeat as requested.

You may have to give help and a number of repetitions for some students at first, because listeners may not have learned to pay attention to deep tones.

Exchange papers, check and record grades.

Repeat the music excerpt once more.

Exercise 5

Music work: Third movement of Beethoven's *Symphony No. 9.*

Excerpt: begin the music on measure 25 at the time the meter changes from 4/4 to 3/4. Play eight measures.

Play the excerpt over once or twice until listeners recognize the theme and meter.

Ask trainees to make a dash pattern of the bass tones which are being played as background for the theme.

The bass pattern is:

$$D \downarrow C^{\#} \overset{\frown}{AA} \uparrow D \downarrow \overset{\frown}{AA} \uparrow E \downarrow \overset{\frown}{AA} \uparrow F^{\#} \downarrow \overset{\frown}{AA}$$

Exchange papers, check and record grades.

Repeat the music once more.

Listeners have customarily responded to the exercises for hearing background effects with momentary feelings of superiority. Their faces light up with surprise and pleasure as they actually hear the sounds in the background. It appears that they feel they are the first listeners to have made the discovery. Since they had never heard the sounds before they had not realized the sounds were there.

The bass pattern in Exercise four often strikes them as somewhat humorous. They comment and laugh about the "industrious and enthusiastic" style in which the pattern is repeated as if the bass sounds were of greatest importance.

The Beethoven music in Exercise five never fails to make a deep and lasting impression on trainees.

CONTRASTING TONE COLORS OF
OBOE AND ENGLISH HORN

Introduce the oboe as the soprano voice of the double reed instruments and the English horn as an alto oboe.

Classes may not be as familiar with the tone color of these two instruments as they are with many others of the orchestra. There are fewer opportunities to hear them alone and identify their tone colors.

Our objective in presenting the exercises is to develop rapid identification of the tone colors and a clear reaction awareness of each. Their unique tone colors are employed for so many important roles by composers and for expressive effects not attainable in other instrumental tone colors.

While listening to recorded music, listeners often confuse oboe with English horn and with clarinet until they become experienced.

Exercise 1

Music work: Third movement of Beethoven's *Symphony No. 6.*

Excerpt: begin the music on measure 91. It comes about one third inch over on the record band where theme three enters in oboe tone color. Play through the first count of measure 122 where the oboe gives up the melody. The meter is 3/4.

Direct students to listen with the objective of identifying tone color of the oboe so clearly that they will recognize it at once whenever it sounds in their hearing range.

Mention that the oboe will be playing the melody above a light string accompaniment.

Play the music several times and review it several times on successive days.

Exercise 2

Music work: Second movement of Beethoven's *Eroica Symphony.*

Excerpt: begin the music where the oboe enters playing the first theme. The movement opens with the strings playing the theme once through. The oboe takes the theme the second time.

Play the excerpt several times and review it on successive days.

Exercise 3

Music work: "The Moldau" by Smetana.

Excerpt: begin the music where the peasant wedding dance enters. It comes three-fifths of an inch over on the record band. There will be no difficulty in finding it because it is the only section of the music suggestive of dancing. Play until the dance music ends.

Write the word *oboe* on the blackboard. Direct listeners to keep their faces turned straight front and to turn their eyes toward the word on the board when they hear the oboe sounds.

The oboe plays a sustained sound in the background which harmonizes with the sounds of the dance melody. It enters soon after the middle of the dance section. The oboe here gives a touch of warm exotic color coming through the melody and other sounds. It makes a pleasing contrast and a moving impression. It adds much to the expression.

It is advisable to check this section of a record when selecting one. If the tonal balance is not good, the beautiful effect of the oboe does not come through and this exercise cannot be presented.

Play the whole dance section through several times and repeat it on successive days.

Exercise 4

Music work: "Largo" from Dvorak's *New World Symphony.*

Excerpt: start the music at the end of the sustained, chordal introduction and play through the first theme.

Ask the students to listen with the aim of learning to identify the English horn tone color as it differs from all others. Suggest that they have special concern for finding the difference between its tone color and the color of oboe tone.

Repeat the music several times and review it on other days several times.

Exercise 5

Music work: "Danse des Mirlitons" (Dance of the Flutes) from Tschaikowsky's *Nut-Cracker Suite.*

Excerpt: start the music after the introduction is completed and the flutes have played the first theme. Play until the flutes enter once more. The English horn plays a singing melody between the flute renditions of theme one.

Teacher A was in a music department where he could bring in capable players of oboe and English horn to demonstrate tone color for the class.

He placed them outside the visual range of listeners and had them alternate with each other in playing for the class. Listeners were asked to write which tone color they heard. He gave them six to eight examples.

The procedure was a substantial aid to trainees in developing identification of each tone color. Reaction awareness developed at the same time.

Teacher B felt that tone color of English horn and oboe each had such obviously different tone texture from most other instruments that he could not pass up the opportunity to begin making listeners conscious of texture even though they were to have a separate presentation of texture later.

When students had identified the sustained oboe tone in the background of the peasant wedding dance, he inquired as to what made it possible to hear the oboe through sounds of a large number of other instruments playing both melody and rhythm at the time the oboe sounds were being heard.

Trainees would listen again, discussion would follow and the reason brought out that the oboe had a sharper edged, penetrating quality which made it capable of "cutting through" the other combined tones. It could become audible even when it was greatly outnumbered.

Teacher B reported that listeners approached the lessons on tone texture in later exercises with greater sensitivity for texture by having gained awareness of it here. It also lead them to take notice of texture during other listening experience.

SCALE MODE IDENTIFICATION THROUGH RECORDED EXCERPTS

Listeners' reaction awareness of scale pattern is important for receiving communication of composers. The exercises presented below are introduced to deepen sensitivity toward scale patterns.

Tell the students that you are going to play music in which the melodies will contain several different kinds of scale patterns. They are to identify the patterns when they are sounded and write the scale name after hearing the music in each exercise. There may be more than one of these patterns in some compositions.

Arrange for writing materials.

Exchange papers, check and record grades on each exercise.

Exercise 1

Music work: "My Heart At Thy Sweet Voice" from *Samson and Delilah* by Saint-Saëns.

Excerpt: begin the music on the refrain where the chromatic scale pattern is clearly in evidence. Play until the refrain is completed.

Repeat as requested.

Exercise 2

Music work: "Largo" from Dvorak's *New World Symphony.*

Excerpt: begin the music after the introduction of chordal passages played by the brass. Play through the first theme.

Give help if necessary in identifying the pentatonic scale pattern.

Repeat as requested.

Exercise 3

Music work: Minuet from Mozart's *Symphony in G Minor.*

Play the entire movement. The first theme and section are in minor, the second in major and the final one in minor again.

Trainees will need to hear the music several times in the average class before they can make a decision. By that time they will have identified Mozart's themes and gained a fair measure of his communication. While they have been listening intently to recognize scale patterns they will have gained reaction awareness of many other sounds of music elements in addition.

CHAPTER SEVEN

Expanding Listener Reaction to Theme, Rhythm, Tone Color and Key

Through the presentation of exercises described in this chapter, an instructor can lead students to greater independence in identification of theme, rhythm motion and tempo, through hearing. Class members gain competency as listeners because what each does in the class experiences can be done by the individual with other music of his choice. He can follow the procedure he experiences in class to learn other music works, free of any aid from the instructor.

The student can broaden his reaction awareness of clarinet tone color and establish sensitivity toward the effect of varied harmonic keys as they are employed by composers.

TEACHING TWO THEMES AND IDENTIFYING THEME IN WRITING

Identification of themes is recognition of the chief subjects of a music work. The following exercises are designed to keep listeners' alert attention on each of the themes every time they are played in the music. This degree of attention is essential because students must identify them rapidly, through hearing, in order to follow the composer's expression as he develops the theme or subject.

Tell the class that in each of the following exercises you are going to review a theme they have heard before. You are going to follow this by presenting a new theme for them to hear and write in dash patterns while they are listening.

When all listeners have identified the themes they are to write a pattern of their interchange with one another. Every time the first theme is heard listeners are to write the letter "A." Every time the second theme is heard they are to write the letter "B."

Arrange for writing materials.

The five exercises to follow are strenuous. One exercise is sufficient on any one day. Each requires exacting response. Gains in hearing accuracy made by the listeners compensate in full for the required effort.

Exercise 1

Music work: Second Movement of Beethoven's *Symphony No. 5.*

Excerpt: play the first eight measures of the music. It is in 3/8 meter.

Introduce the theme as a review of one they have heard before during an exercise for recognition of viola tone color. ·

Allow students to decide whether they feel sure they can identify the theme or if they think they need to write a dash pattern to secure it. Proceed according to their needs.

Most students can identify it easily without making the dash patterns.

Exercise 2

Music work: Second Movement of Beethoven's *Symphony No. 5.*

Excerpt: begin the music on measure 22 where the second theme enters on the third beat. Play through the first beat of measure 31.

Direct students to write a dash pattern of this, the second theme of the music work which they are to hear.

Repeat as requested, but urge them to complete the pattern as soon as possible.

Exchange papers, check and record grades.

Exercise 3

Music work: Second Movement of Beethoven's *Symphony No. 5.*

Excerpt: play the first 90 measures of the music which will include the following theme pattern:

Theme A
Theme B
Theme A with variations
Theme B
Theme B

Instruct listeners to write the letter representing the theme only when the whole theme is heard. If there is only a part of the theme sounded they are not to count it or write the letter.

Some listeners may feel uncertain about recognizing the "A" theme in variations. They may require some help from the instructor in identifying it as the "A" theme.

Play as requested.

While students are experiencing the repeated hearings, they are developing an aural image of this music, so treasured among all music works.

Exchange papers, check and record grades.

Repeat the excerpt once more.

Exercise 4

Music work: First Movement of Schubert's *Unfinished Symphony.*

Excerpt: begin the music on the 11th measure of this 3/4 meter, where the oboe enters playing theme one. Before that the 'cellos and bass viols have played an introduction melody and the violins have played two measures of an accompanying motive.

Play through theme one.

Ask the students to make a dash pattern of the theme as they listen.

Repeat as requested.

Tell the class you are going to play the second theme in review. They will remember having heard it in the exercises on 'cello tone color in Chapter 5.

Repeat several times.

Direct students to write an A, B theme pattern as they did in Exercise 3. Begin the music on measure 11 and play through the following theme pattern:

Theme A in oboe tone color.

Theme A with extension on theme.

Theme B in 'cello tone color and with an extension on the theme.

Theme B in violin tone color.

After papers are checked and recorded, play the music again and ask listeners to identify the instruments they heard playing each theme each time.

Ask them to identify the meter and tempo.

Play the music from the beginning and let trainees find that they already know the introduction melody. They learned it in the exercises on low string tone color.

Exercise 5

Music work: Roumanian Rhapsody, No. 1 by Georges Enesco.

Excerpt: begin the music at the first of the record band and play through themes I A and I B up to where theme 2 enters.

The themes are from a Roumanian folk song, "Land of Sunshine." You may want to teach the class to sing it and make listeners familiar with the themes in this way, or have them write dash patterns for each one.

Enesco cut the note durations and increased the tempo of the themes when he adopted them for his composition. Theme 1 A is two measures long and theme I B is three measures in length The meter is in common time.

When students have identified both themes, direct them to listen to the excerpt and write a pattern of the themes as they did in exercise 3. The theme pattern is as follows:

A A B B A A B A A B B.

Repeat as requested.

Exchange papers, check and record grades.

Play the music once more.

DEVELOPING IDENTIFICATION WITH MOTION AND TEMPO

Listeners who have not yet gained ability to identify tempo through awareness of the speed with which primary accents occur in succession can be thrown into confusion by all but the very obvious rhythm sounds. The exercises to follow are designed to instill the habit in listeners of recognizing the tempo by primary accents and identifying in perception and feeling with both the meter motion and tempo.

The listener must learn to accept the tempo in the very first measures of the music. He must abstractly experience the motion of the rhythm at the tempo being expressed at any given time in the music performance.

Explain to students that a competent listener, of his own volition, grants his attention at the tempo of the composer.

To demonstrate, ask listeners to hum the theme we tagged "Russian theme" from *Capriccio Italien,* while you mark the accented beats on the desk. Call attention to the fact that the tempo is suggestive of slow, heavy-hearted walking steps.

Ask them to hum the theme we tagged "tarantella theme" from the same music while you mark the accents on the desk.

Establish realization that a listener whose mental processes were responding at the tempo of the first example would be left far behind if the music being sounded came at the speed of the second example.

Mention as an added example that an individual may hear and gain some communication from a lullaby while he is drifting along in a mental state of reverie because the tempo is slow. In the same state music with sounds of loud brass and percussion will jolt him out of the reverie and impose the expression and tempo on him, willing or not. The listener is not able to respond in a state of reverie to music of the tempo and complexity of a symphony first movement and gain its communication. In such a state he probably experiences only confusion and irritation because the music stimulates reactions much faster than he is identifying them and receiving their expression.

Tell students you are going to play excerpts of music in a variety of tempos with the purpose of developing their ability to recognize at once meter motion and tempo.

Arrange for writing materials.

Instruct listeners to write the number of beats in a measure on each excerpt. They are to write an identification of the tempo as:

Slow, medium, fast or very rapid.

In addition, instruct trainees to write at the end of each excerpt a suggested common motion to which the meter motion is similar. Some suggested ones are:

Slow heavy steps
Average walking speed
Brisk walking speed
Urgent walking speed
Running speed

Do not permit any overt physical response, not even finger-tapping on desks while they are doing the exercises. The motion and tempo are to be experienced abstractly. Explain that any overt motion can become an interference with other class members.

In rapid tempos, adequate physical response would not be possible. Trainees are capable, at this stage of training, of identifying with motion and tempo without making physical response.

Exercise 1

Music work: First Movement of Beethoven's *Symphony No. 5.*

Excerpt: begin at the first of the music and play through measure 21 where the pause note is heard. The meter is 2/4.

Students often judge it similar in motion to a very brisk walk, or an urgent walking speed.

Repeat as requested.

Exchange papers, check and record grades.

Repeat the music after writing the name of the first movement on the blackboard, "Allegro Con Brio." Explain its meaning to the class and tell the students they are expected to remember the term and its meaning.

Exercise 2

Music work: Second Movement of Beethoven's *Symphony No. 5.*

Excerpt: begin at the first of the movement and play 19 measures. The music is in 3/8 meter.

Listeners most often judge it similar in motion and tempo to a lively walk.

Repeat as requested.

Exchange papers, check and record grades.

Repeat the music after writing the name, "Andante Con Moto," on the blackboard, and requesting that they memorize the words and their meaning.

Exercise 3

Music work: Third Movement of Beethoven's *Symphony No. 5.*

Excerpt: begin the music on measure 19.

The ritards and pauses in earlier measures make it difficult for trainees to identify the meter. Play through the first beat of measure 46. The music is in 3/4 meter.

Listeners most often judge it similar to running steps in motion and tempo.

Repeat as requested.

Exchange papers, check and record grades.

Repeat the music after writing the name, "Allegro," on the blackboard and requesting that they memorize the word and its meaning.

Exercise 4

Music work: Fourth Movement of Beethoven's *Symphony No. 5.*

Excerpt: begin the music at the first of the movement. Customarily the third and fourth movements are played on the same record band. The fourth one begins about one inch over on the band. The meter is common time. Play 18 measures.

Trainees most often judge it as similar in motion and tempo to running steps.

Repeat as requested.

Exchange papers, check and record grades.

Repeat the music after writing the name, "Allegro," on the blackboard.

Exercise 5

Music work: First Movement of Mozart's *Symphony No. 39.*

Excerpt: start the music after the end of the adagio introduction. It ends about one third inch over on the record band and the allegro tempo begins as theme one enters. The meter changes from common time to 3/4 time there. Play through measure 14 of the 3/4 meter.

Students most often judge it as similar in motion and tempo to easy running steps or a hurried minuet.

Repeat as requested.

Exchange papers, check and record grades.

Repeat the excerpt after writing the name of the movement, "Adagio—Allegro," on the blackboard, and instruct students to memorize the word "Adagio" and its meaning.

Exercise 6

Music work: Second Movement of Mozart's *Symphony No. 39.*

Excerpt: begin the music at the first of the movement and play through 16 measures. The meter is 3/4.

Listeners most often judge it as similar to a moderate walking speed.

Repeat as requested.

Exchange papers, check and record grades.

Repeat the excerpt after writing the name of the movement, "Andante," on the blackboard.

Exercise 7

Music work: Third Movement of Mozart's *Symphony No. 39.*

Excerpt: begin at the first of the movement and play through count 1 of measure 16. The music is in 3/4 meter.

Students most often judge it as similar to an energetic minuet in motion and tempo.

Repeat as requested.

Exchange papers, check and record grades.

Repeat the excerpt after writing the name of the movement, "Minuet (Allegretto) and Trio," on the blackboard, and requesting students to memorize the words and their meaning.

Exercise 8

Music work: Fourth Movement of Mozart's *Symphony No. 39.*

Excerpt: begin at the first of the music and play through 16 measures. The meter is 2/4.

Listeners most often judge it as similar to animated running steps in motion and tempo.

Repeat as requested.

Exchange papers, check and record grades.

Repeat the music after writing the name of the movement, "Allegro," on the blackboard.

Teacher A made a practice of asking trainees to listen to the excerpts from exercises one and five with the purpose of discovering differences in the rhythm expression between the allegros of Beethoven and Mozart.

He led them to recognize a vigor and emotional intensity in Beethoven's music, which was different from the serenity and feeling of weightless freedom in Mozart's music.

He found they had more difficulty expressing their observations of the second movements which were presented in exercises 2 and 6. They identified the difference in meter. Some would point out the greater emotional intensity in Beethoven's expression in the "Andante." Others would mention the upward soaring motion of the higher strings with a suggestion of serenity in the Mozart music.

A few would express awareness of Beethoven's different employment of the bass tones at a deeper range which he used to make accents and to express deeper emotional expression. Mozart, they found, used a more sustained bass with harmonic effects.

The excerpts from exercises 3 and 7 generally brought out comments on the vigorous, almost rough, intensity of expression in Beethoven's rhythm, which contrasted with the animation and joyousness of Mozart's expression.

The excerpts from exercises 4 and 8 brought such descriptions as Beethoven's rhythm being suggestive of vigor, exuberance and achievement of victory. Mozart's rhythm was described as rollicking motion with superanimation.

Teacher B followed the exercises for identifying motion and tempo with short reviews over an extended time. At class activity interludes for changes from one type to another, he would introduce 8 to 16 measures of the opening bars of a new music selection and ask students to identify the meter motion and tempo. He found that it increased rapid awareness of these aspects of expression.

TRANSPOSING A FAMILIAR MELODY TO DEMONSTRATE EFFECT OF KEYS

Our objective in presenting the exercises on the effect of keys is to awaken reaction awareness of the difference in musical expression due to selection of key.

Mention to listeners that composers choose key with great care and with strong conviction that one certain key best expresses what they wish to communicate.

A melody can be and often is transposed into keys other than the authentic one. This may be done in order to fit a given voice range or because performers find some keys easier to play than others. Establish understanding that the expression of a composer is altered to some degree by changing the music to another key. Listeners will come closest to gaining the authentic communication of a composer by hearing his music in the key of the composer's choice.

Exercises are designed to be played on the piano because the music would not be available played in many different keys in recorded version.

Accurate tuning of the piano and the quality of the instrument will have an effect on the quality of the presentation.

If an instructor is not trained in transposing on the keyboard, he may find a pianist who will play examples to be recorded on tape or disc.

Exercise 1

Music work: Brahm's "Lullaby."

Excerpt: begin the music on the first of the melody and play for 16 measures in the key of E^b, which is the original one.

Play the excerpt several times.

Mentally change the key signature to four sharps and play the same 16 measures in the key of E.

Repeat once or more and then play it again in E^b.

Develop a discussion about the effect of the keys in comparison with one another as they express the music.

Listeners are usually quick to discern that the key of E^b has a more mellow expression with tenderness more suitable for a lullaby than the key of E which is a trifle harsh and bright.

Exercise 2

Music work: "O No, John!" an English folk song.

Excerpt: play the first 12 measures in the key of G.

Read the words of the song to the class to give understanding of its humor and the character of the girl speaking.

Repeat the excerpt in the key of G several times.

Mentally change the key signature from one sharp to 6 flats and play the excerpt several times in G flat.

The change made by the key of G flat is soon obvious to listeners. They decide at once that the flat key is dull in comparison with the key of G for expressing the mood of this song.

Exercise 3

Follow a similar procedure with several other selections. Suggested ones are:

"Finiculi Finicula," by Luigi Denza
Play it in D and D^b.

Students immediately observe that the key of D is brighter and more suitable for the gay, carefree mood of the song.

"The Star Spangled Banner," by Francis Scott Key.
Play it in A^b and A.

The key of A is voted more suitable for the bright, patriotic mood.

"Down in the Valley," an American folk song.

Play it in F and then F$^{\#}$.

Students find the key of F more suitable for the sentimental mood of the song.

Listeners discover that keys with flat signatures have a sweeter, more accurately satisfying effect than keys with sharp signatures. The latter are brighter and more active-sounding. The composer selects his key according to which characteristics are more suited to his expression.

Explain to trainees that the sharp of one tone, when accurate, is not identical with the flat of the tone above it. This can be clearly demonstrated on the violin.

Instruments with a set pitch, such as the piano, are made so that the tone of one black key must serve as the sharp of one tone and the flat of the tone above it. The piano tuner must make a compromise on whether he will make the flats accurate, or the sharps. When he chooses to make flats accurate, which is the customary choice, he must do so at the expense of making the sharps more inaccurate. This is the reason why keys with flat signatures have the more soothing, sweet tones and satisfying effect.

The keys of B and E are generally considered to be the brightest keys and to be a trifle harsh for certain moods. They are especially good for expressing vigor, zest, excitement, grandeur, etc. They lack tenderness and emotional expression.

PRESENTING TONE COLORS
OF THE CLARINETS

Most listeners will be familiar with the tone colors of the clarinets for they are played in bands, popular orchestras and often in solo performances. They are heard in flexible rapid motion and in beautiful legato style.

Our objective in the exercises to be presented is to awaken listener reaction awareness of the tone colors by hearing them in sustained legato tones.

Present the clarinet as the dramatic soprano of the woodwind section. Its roles in orchestral music are widely varied with solos, accompaniments and effective embellishments which are not possible on many other instruments.

Ask students to listen with the aim of identifying clarinet tones sufficiently well to recognize them instantaneously whenever they hear clarinet sounds.

Direct them to consider how clarinet tones differ from oboe and flute tones.

Display a poster-size picture of the clarinets.

Exercise 1

Music work: Fourth Movement of Dvorak's *New World Symphony.*

Excerpt: begin the music about one-third inch over on the record band where theme two enters in clarinet tone color accompanied by tremelo sounds from the strings. Play until the music leaves theme two.

Play the excerpt several times and review it on successive days.

This excerpt has proved very effective in developing reaction awareness of the tone color. The legato style and the range give the performer a chance to demonstrate the rich, full-toned expression possible on the instrument.

Exercise 2

Music work: "Scherzo," from Dvorak's *New World Symphony.*

Excerpt: begin the music about one-fourth inch over on the record band where theme two enters in clarinet tone color. This comes after theme two has been heard once from flute and oboe tone colors. Play until 'cello and bassoon take over the theme.

Play the excerpt several times and review it on successive days.

Exercise 3

Introduce the bass clarinet as the deep-toned woodwind with the greatest carrying power and flowing legato style. It has a unique tone color which makes it easy to identify.

Ask class members to compare it with English horn and tuba tone colors while they are listening, with the aim of gaining an instantaneous recognition of its tone whenever they hear it.

Music work: "Dance of the Sugar Plum Fairy," from *Nutcracker Suite* by Tschaikowsky.

Play the entire selection.

Tell listeners that the bass clarinet plays an alternating part with the English horn in the lower tonal range. The celesta is playing bell-like tones above them.

Play the selection several times and review it on other days.

Exercise 4

Music work: "Coronation Marche—Le Prophete" by Meyerbeer.

Play the entire selection.

Write the name "bass clarinet" on the blackboard. Ask listeners to keep faces turned front, but to turn their eyes toward the words on the board when they hear the bass clarinet tones.

Repeat the music.

Review it on other days.

Exercise 5

Music work: "La Fiesta Mexicana," by H. Owen Reed.

Excerpt: play the contra-bass clarinet solo which depicts the stillness of the night before the "Fiesta" begins.

Write the name "contra=bass clarinet" on the blackboard. Ask students to compare it with sounds of the bass clarinet while they listen.

Repeat the music.

Review it on several other days.

CHAPTER EIGHT

Employing Contrasts to Sharpen Awareness of Reaction to Theme, Rhythm and Harmony

An average listening trainee will require further exposure to string tone color in order to activate and deepen his reaction to the sounds of string instruments. Instructors will find the exercises to follow effective in filling this student need.

Contrast has proved very helpful for sustaining listening concentration. The differences between one string tone and another are not so obvious as those between strings and brass or woodwinds. While listening for the subtle differences between strings the individual receives impressive exposure to their sounds.

Listening guides have the objective of leading each trainee to discover for himself the special potential of string tones. They, more than most musical instruments, bring him to awareness of responses in his own feelings and perceptions which set him apart as a human being.

One cannot reach this objective by telling him this fact. He can only be led to the discovery of it through his own experiences.

115

After achieving the objective, you can point out to him that composers have demonstrated knowledge of the special string contribution. Those who have created the most enduring and profound musical expressions have given the most important and continuous role to the string section of the orchestra.

In exercises for uneven rhythm recognition, those for hearing dissonance and consonance, and those for distinguishing tone colors of two woodwinds, the teacher will find use of contrast a substantial aid. It guides students to hear components of a given music element through observing how those components differ from one another.

HEARING EXCERPTS WITH STRING CONTRASTS AND MAKING IDENTIFICATIONS

The exercises in this section are strenuous. One on any given day will be adequate.

Explain to the class that you are going to present music which has contrasting string tone colors. Ask the students to identify the tone color they hear by writing the name of the instrument being sounded on the melody and those being sounded in the background.

Arrange for writing materials.

Exercise 1

Music work: Slow movement from the "Emperor String Quartet," Opus 76, No. 3, by Haydn.

Play through variation one.

Mention to trainees that the theme is from *The Austrian National Anthem,* which Haydn wrote in 1797 and presented to that nation.

In the first variation the melody is played in the second violin part, while the first violin plays a staccato accompaniment in arpeggios.

Repeat as requested.

Exchange papers, check and record grades.

Repeat the music once more.

Exercise 2

Music work: Slow movement from the "Emperor String Quartet," by Haydn.

Play through variation 2.

The melody is played on 'cello.

The second violin is played on a counter melody, while the first violin and viola are heard in the accompaniment.

Repeat as requested.

Exchange papers, check, and record grades.

Repeat the music once more.

Exercise 3

Music work: Slow movement from the "Emperor String Quartet," by Haydn.

Play through variation 3.

The theme is played on viola; 'cello and violin are played on a counterpart in the background.

Repeat as requested.

Exchange papers, check, and record grades.

Repeat the music once more.

Exercise 4

Music work: Slow movement from the "Emperor String Quartet," by Haydn.

Play through variation 4.

The violin is played on the melody.

Repeat as requested.

Exchange papers, check and record grades.

Repeat the music once more.

Exercise 5

Music work: Britten's "Young People's Guide to the Orchestra."

Play through variation 8.

The melody is played on the double bass. Woodwind sounds are played in the background.

Repeat as requested.

Exchange papers, check and record grades.

Repeat the music again.

Exercise 6

Music work: Britten's "Young People's Guide to the Orchestra."

Play through variation 6.

The melody is played on the viola. Woodwinds and brasses are played in the background.

Repeat as requested.
Exchange papers, check and record grades.

Exercise 7

Music work: Britten's "Young People's Guide to the Orchestra."
Play through variation 7.
The melody is played on 'cello. Viola and clarinet tone colors are played in the background.
Repeat as requested.
Exchange papers, check and record grades.
Repeat the music again.

Exercise 8

Music work: Britten's "Young People's Guide to the Orchestra."
Play through variation 5.
The melody is played on violins.
Brass tones are played in the background.
Repeat as requested.
Exchange papers, check and record grades.
Repeat the music again.

Teacher A reported that he presented only four of these exercises with the first group he taught. With each succeeding group he added more. As he gained evidence of their effectiveness he began to present all of them and even to review a few.

Teacher B was a performer in string quartet. He achieved enviable success with a chamber music listening club of college students. He made a practice of following up the exercises by making brief, surprise presentations of one or another excerpt from them. At the end of an activity he would play an excerpt and expect students to rapidly identify the string tone they were hearing on both melody and background sounds.

Teacher C related that he presented the first four exercises in one class period because he arranged to have the recording for only a short time. He discovered that listeners became fatigued and inattentive even though he considered them an exceptionally good class.

Teacher D had a superb advantage, which most teachers could not duplicate. He was permitted to seat his listening trainees behind screens during symphony rehearsals and have them listen.

The symphony orchestra rehearsed in a campus hall. One hour of hearing live, the buoyant, musical string tones of professional musicians did more to awaken reaction awareness of tone color than weeks of class presentation could ever do.

Students had to sit behind screens to be sure they would not interfere with rehearsal. This proved an advantage for listeners because they did not divide their attention between listening and watching the performers.

A consideration of the series of eight exercises described above may indicate an excessive drill on string tone color. If presented one after the other they become just that. Listeners cannot give such intensive attention over a long time span as the exercises require. However, the exercises are interspersed between other activities and presented with a day or two intervening, they are tremendously effective.

Keep in mind that listeners must give more attention to hearing string tone than is required by more obvious instrumental tones. Instruments which have penetrating tone or an inescapable impact on the hearing nerves are heard with much less attention. There has been little progress made in gaining reaction awareness of string tone by urging the listener to pay more attention and concentrate more. Repeated exposure to string tones, contrasted in short presentations, has brought very satisfying results.

DEMONSTRATING MOTION IN UNEVEN
RHYTHM – RUBATO, ETC.

Trainees have learned to recognize tempo by responding to successive primary accents of music to which they are listening. They have also learned to feel the motion of the music meter in imagination and to sense the motion in the abstract. One objective in the exercises to follow is to extend student sensitivity to where they respond spontaneously to an increase or decrease in tempo when either occurs in the music.

Write three terms on the blackboard—accelerando, ritardando and rubato tempo—leave a wide space between them.

Explain the meaning of each term. Ask students to suggest motions from everyday experiences which fit each term. The following are some frequently suggested:

Accelerando:

> Students hurrying to class as time for the tardy bell draws near.
>
> Students moving toward the school cafeterias at lunch time.

Ritardando:

> Students approaching a test area.
>
> Students leaving a recreation area to return to class.

Rubato Tempo:

> Resembles the childhood game of "Follow the Leader" because of its unpredictable changes.

Mention that emotions often cause tempo changes in the speech of individuals. Stress, excitement or anger may hasten the tempo, while sorrow, tenderness or uncertainty may slow it down. In exactly the same way a composer may resort to increasing or decreasing tempo to more vividly express his feelings.

Rubato· tempo appears most often in music of countries where the gypsy peoples have exerted their influence on musical expression. They have widely employed this tempo in their dances which often include surprise changes of tempo. One of the popular dances is the "Czardas," in which tempo alternates between slow and rapid motion. There are many leaps and much twirling in their dances, all of which is reflected in the music.

Liszt, Enesco, Strauss and Brahms have used rubato tempo frequently.

Tell listeners you are going to present music which includes the tempo changes created in music to further emotional expression.

Tell them that each musical example will contain one of the three tempo alterations which you have been discussing. Ask them to try to identify with the rhythm in imagining motion and to continue to do this as the tempo becomes faster or slower.

Exercise 1

Music work: "Danse Bohème," from *Carmen Suite* by Bizet.
Excerpt: begin the music at the first and play through the first theme once. This will permit listeners to recognize the 3/4 meter

in regular motion and tempo. Students will remember the theme from a previous exercise on accent in Chapter 6.

Move over to the final third of the record band and let trainees hear the accelerando to the end of the selection.

Direct listeners to keep faces turned front and to turn their eyes toward the word "accelerando" as they hear the tempo continue to increase.

Repeat the last excerpt at least three times.

Exercise 2

Music work: Third Movement of Beethoven's *Symphony No. 5.*

Excerpt: begin the music about one-fourth inch on the record band before the end of the movement. The students will have a chance to detect the regular tempo and motion before the accelerando begins. The music is in 3/4 meter.

Direct trainees to turn their eyes toward the word "accelerando" when they hear the tempo continue to increase and to keep faces turned straight front.

Repeat the excerpt several times.

Exercise 3

Music work: "Capriccio Italien," by Tschaikowsky.

Excerpt: begin the music about one-half inch before the end of the record band, where the imitation bagpipe sounds enter. Play through the very obvious ritardando and up to the entrance of "Italian theme No. 1."

Ask students to keep faces turned straight front and to turn their eyes to the word *ritardando* on the board when they hear the tempo continue to slow down.

Repeat the example several times.

Exercise 4

Music work: Second Movement of Dvorak's *New World Symphony.*

Excerpt: begin the music about one-third inch from the end of the record band and play to the end.

Introduce the excerpt as an example of ritardando and ask listeners to turn their eyes to that word on the board when they hear the tempo and motion slow down. Faces are to be kept straight front.

Repeat the excerpt several times.

Exercise 5

Music work: "Roumanian Rhapsody" by Georges Enesco.

Excerpt: begin at the first of the music and play until the strings enter on theme two in an upward sweep.

Introduce the excerpt as an example of rubato tempo, and request listeners to turn their eyes toward those words on the board when they hear the tempo increase and decrease alternately.

Repeat the excerpt at least three times and more if requested.

Exercise 6

Music work: "Hungarian Dance No. 5" by Brahms. Play the whole selection.

Warn listeners to pay exacting attention to tempo and meter because gypsy music is so complex that a student can mistake other exciting expression with tempo variation and then become confused in identifying the actual rubato tempo. The meter is 2/4.

Again request students to keep faces turned straight front and to turn eyes toward the words on the board whenever they hear the rubato tempo.

Repeat the music twice.

Exercise 7

Music work: "Hungarian Rhapsody No. 2" by Liszt.

This music contains numerous examples of rubato tempo. Since the location of the most obvious excerpts varies with the interpretation by different conductors, the choice of excerpts will be left to the instructor.

Choose three excerpts, two with even tempo and one with rubato tempo. Ask students to identify each, in writing, as even tempo or rubato.

Exchange papers, check and record grades.

Repeat the excerpts once each.

Exercise 8

Music work: "Village Swallows" by Strauss.

Follow the same procedure as used in Exercise 7.

Students enjoy the above exercises. They seem to react to them as recreation rather than as studies.

DISSONANCE AND CONSONANCE

Our objective in presenting exercises on dissonance and consonance is to develop a sensitive listener response to their sounds. The trainee becomes involved in experiences of hearing each one and becoming aware that each affects his hearing senses in a different way. First we help him to recognize each one. Second we lead him to discover the interaction between them, which is similar to that of active tones in relation to rest tones.

Explain to students that dissonance and consonance are heard to a greater or lesser degree in most music. Their role in musical expression is an important part of composer expression. You are going to play examples of each for them to hear and learn to identify.

Tell listeners that dissonance moves to consonance in order to sound complete just as active tones move to rest tones. Ask them to be especially attentive to the active and rest effects in the exercises they hear.

Exercise 1

Play each of the following intervals on the piano as examples of consonance:

G E G C A A^b
C C E C C C

Establish student recognition that these tones sound pleasing and satisfying. They are stable and complete, requiring no other tones to follow.

Repeat the examples once or twice.

Exercise 2

Play the following examples, with appropriate pauses between, as examples of dissonance:

G$^\#$ B B B F
G A F C B

Establish recognition that these tones sound both incomplete and irritating.

Repeat each chord several times.

Exercise 3

Tell students you are going to play the dissonance tones from exercise 2, followed by chords of consonance to demonstrate the satisfying result from the chord of resolution. This is the consonant chord which follows the dissonant one.

Play

G$^\#$	A		B	B		B	C
G	F$^\#$		A	G$^\#$		F	E
	B	A		F	E		
	C	F		B	C		

Establish recognition that the unrest and harshness of the dissonant tones are dissolved in the restful effect of the consonant tones.

Repeat the examples.

Exercise 4

Play the following chord progression on the piano. It is one Beethoven employed in his "Moonlight Sonata." He presented the harmony in broken chords:

B	C	A$^\#$	B
F$^\#$	G	G	F$^\#$
D$^\#$	E	E	D$^\#$
B	B	B	B

Play the first three chords once and hesitate before the fourth chord of resolution to allow listeners to feel the tremendous drive toward the final consonant sounds.

Repeat the example several times.

Mention to students that the skilled composer takes care to create a balance between consonance and dissonance in order to retain the interest of his listeners. If he uses consonance excessively the listeners find the music dull or tiresome. Such music becomes so inactive and restful that the listeners doze.

If the composer uses dissonance to excess, the listeners may become irritated and withdraw interest. The music seems to be taking forever to complete the expression. In this case, the music seems meaningless.

Exercise 5

Music work: "Finlandia" by Sibelius.

Excerpt: play the opening section where the chords furnish an excellent example of dissonance.

Repeat the excerpt several times.

Exercise 6

Music work: "Anitra's Dance" from *Peer Gynt Suite* by Grieg.

Excerpt: begin the music at the first and play through the first beat of measure 55. The music is in 3/4 meter.

Write the word "consonant" on the blackboard. Ask students to keep faces toward front, but to turn their eyes toward the word on the board when they hear the music move to a consonant chord and repose momentarily.

There are approximately nine places where this happens.

Repeat as requested.

Grade students on these responses to make sure that they give the necessary effort.

INTRODUCING PICCOLO AND FLUTE

Introduce piccolo tone color as the bright light of the woodwind section. It has one of the instrumental colors which gains rapid reaction awareness in short exposure time. The flute, in its lower and middle range, requires a longer exposure to develop reaction awareness. It is easily confused with clarinet tone when heard from recordings.

Our objective in presenting the exercises with these tone colors is to develop rapid identification of them in the higher range, and to develop deeper reaction awareness of flute tone color.

Special care must be taken in regulating the volume of tones when presenting these instruments. If it is too subdued the tone will not be authentic. If the volume is too loud the piccolo in ˝ particular can be offensive. Then its tone seems harsh and shrieking.

Exercise 1

Music work: "La Garde Montante" from *Carmen Suite* by Bizet.

Excerpt: begin the music where the distant and close-up bugle calls end. Play through the theme three times.

Present the music as an example of piccolo tone color.

Play the excerpt several times and review it on another day.

Exercise 2

Music work: "Chinese Dance" from *Nutcracker Suite* by Tschaikowsky.

Play the entire selection.

Present the music as an example of flute and piccolo tone colors.

Explain to the class that flute and piccolo are combined in much of this music. You want them to listen especially for the places where the piccolo plays a different part from the flute.

Write the word "piccolo" on the blackboard and direct trainees to keep faces front, but to turn eyes toward the name on the board when they hear an added part from the piccolo.

Repeat as requested.

Review on other days.

Exercise 3

Introduce the flute as the coloratura soprano of the woodwind section.

Music work: "Intermezzo" from *Carmen Suite* by Bizet.

Excerpt: begin the music after the short broken-chord introduction played on the harp.

Play through the theme twice.

Ask students to make a dash pattern of the theme. This offers an opportunity to repeat the excerpt many times and lengthens the exposure time to flute tone color.

Repeat as requested.

Review on successive days.

Exercise 4

Music work: "Afternoon of a Faun" by Debussy.

Excerpt: begin the music at the first of the record band and play through the theme twice.

Introduce the excerpt as an example of flute tone color.

This presentation of the flute tone color has proved most effective for developing reaction awareness in the listener.

Question students and establish recognition of the chromatic scale pattern heard in the theme. Ask them to identify the count in each measure. Each has nine counts.

Repeat the music several times and review it on other days.

CHAPTER NINE

Developing Advanced Reaction Awareness
of Harmony, and Tone Quality
Dynamic Effects

Exercises described in this chapter are for listening trainees who have developed advanced skills. An instructor who has led his students to a level of ability which makes them capable of doing these exercises merits a feeling of great pride in his accomplishment. This is especially true if he looks back in memory to the time when students were struggling to make basic identifications of each music element heard in fairly simple and obvious sounds. Success with the following listening activities brings an added measure of satisfaction and greater understanding of musical expression.

PRESENTING BASSOON AND CONTRA-BASSOON
TONE COLORS

Introduce the bassoon as the bass voice of the double reed woodwind section, and the contra-bassoon as the deepest toned instrument of the entire orchestra.

Listeners are often unfamiliar with the tone color of either bassoon. These instruments are not frequently heard alone when they can be clearly identified. Once listeners have identified their unique tone color they rarely confuse it with that of any other instrument.

During future experiences the student will hear bassoon tone color with the instrument's facility for expressing humor and a wide variety of musical effects. In the exercises of the present chapter our chief objective is to develop trainee reaction awareness of the tone color. The exercises have been designed to give extended exposure to the obvious tone color so as to rapidly achieve our goal.

Request students to listen with the purpose of establishing a clear aural image of bassoon tone color so that they can rapidly identify it from that of every other instrument.

Display a poster-sized picture of each bassoon.

Exercise 1

Music work: Third Movement of Gustav Mahler's *Symphony No. 1.*

Excerpt: begin the music after the completion of the introduction and the playing of the first theme on the bass viol. The bassoon enters on the theme as it comes the second time through.

Listeners will remember the theme from the song, "Brother John," and from their previous exercises on tone color of the bass viol and tuba.

Repeat the bassoon theme several times, and review it on other days.

Exercise 2

Music work: "American Salute" by Morton Gould.

Excerpt: begin the music at the close of the introduction where the theme enters in bassoon tone color. The theme is from the song "When Johnny Comes Marching Home."

Play through the theme.

Repeat the excerpt a number of times and review it another day.

Exercise 3

Music work: Third Movement of Beethoven's *Symphony No. 8*

Excerpt: begin the music about halfway over on the record band where theme two enters in bassoon tone color.

Play through the theme a number of times.
Review it on other days.

Exercise 4

Music work: Bolero by Ravel.

Excerpt: begin the music where the flute and then the clarinet have completed the "A" theme. At that place, the bassoon enters on the "B" theme.

Play until the clarinet takes the theme again.

Play the excerpt several times and review it on other days.

Exercise 5

Music work: "In the Hall of the Mountain King." from *Peer Gynt Suite* by Grieg.

Play the entire selection.

Write the word "bassoon" on the blackboard. Ask trainees to keep faces turned straight front, but to turn their eyes toward the word on the board whenever they hear bassoon tone color.

Repeat the music twice.

Exercise 6

Music works: Two band selections:

"La Fiesta Mexicana" by H. Owen Reed, and Fourth Movement of *Symphony For Band* by Vincent Persichetti.

Ask students to listen especially for tone color contrasts between brasses and woodwinds.

CHOICE EXCERPTS OF HARMONIC EFFECTS

Excerpts included in this section have been chosen from a list of experimental ones which were employed in order to effect direct communication from composer to listener through sounds of harmony.

The one remaining aspect of harmony to be featured is that of balance of tones sounded in the various parts of the harmonic structure. Our objective in presenting this aspect is to guide listeners to recognize the bass tones as the foundation upon which the structure stands. Students usually require more experience in attending to bass tones than they have been subjected to heretofore. In each exercise special attention will be given to this matter the first time they listen to the excerpt.

The success of the presentation for balance will depend upon the recordings and equipment used for production and their volume in relation to the size of the listening room. When the volume is turned up too loud for the area, in order to acquire tonal balance, all our efforts fail, for the loud volume creates a negative response in our listeners who automatically try to escape hearing. If the volume is too subdued, the low tones fade out and the harmony goes off balance through loss of its foundation. This matter poses a problem which each instructor must try his utmost to solve if the objective is to be achieved.

Response to these excerpts on harmony has become a source of deep satisfaction for all teachers and a memorable, very meaningful experience for trainees.

Inform the class that you are going to present music excerpts in which the element of harmony plays a very important role in composer expression. Direct the students to give special attention to the sounds of harmony. Tell them you are turning over to them the whole responsibility for attending to the sounds. There will be no response in writing or turning the eyes toward an identifying word, because you are satisfied that they have advanced beyond need for that help from you.

Explain briefly that the bass tones are the foundation which gives stability and balance to the harmonic structure created in the higher voices. Ask them to give special attention to the bass tones the first time they listen to each excerpt.

Exercise 1

Music work: "Jesu, Joy of Man's Desiring," instrumental version, by Bach.

Play through the selection.

Mention to listeners that Bach, in this music, keeps a feeling of tonal balance in the harmony through the full-toned bass foundation.

Before the second hearing ask trainees to notice that when the higher tones soar upward, when their carrying power increases, Bach increases the bass tones to balance them. At the same time there comes a greater contrast between the lush lower tones and the brighter high tones. They complement one another to the listeners' pleasure. Together they more than double the expression each would give alone.

Exercise 2

Music work: "The Moldau" by Smetana.

Excerpt: play through the peasant wedding section.

After the music has been heard once, call attention to the way the regular bass marks the accents and gives vigor to the rhythm motion. In addition there is a much deeper contra-bass playing at the same time. It is important for trainees to hear and react with awareness to it, because it greatly expands the feeling expression. It contrasts and enhances at the same time the tones sounded in higher range.

Exercise 3

Music work: "Wedding Day at Troldhagen" by Grieg.

Play through the selection.

Mention that Grieg uses dissonance often in his harmony. Play the music.

Before you repeat the music conduct a short discussion to see what they have observed while listening to it.

Lead them to recognize that Grieg uses a tremendous volume in the bass which is deeply moving on the emotions. It could become a somber roaring sound if it were not combined with the vibrant higher tones. The bright, gay mood of the wedding celebration comes through with the vigor of motion in higher tones, contrasting with the heavy bass ones.

Repeat the music at least once more.

Exercise 4

Music work: Third Movement of Beethoven's *Symphony No. 9.*

Excerpt: begin on measure 25 and play through measure 41.

The students will be familiar with the excerpt from hearing it in previous exercises. Most of them will have already formed a sharp aural image of this music, but now we want them to get the full impact of the harmonic progression as well.

Play through the excerpt once and point out that Beethoven uses the bass in a less obvious role than do Grieg and Bach, but it is there all of the time as an unobtrusive, but substantial foundation. It adds emotional depth. Bass contrast with the high string and woodwind sounds adds greatly to the meaningful expression.

Repeat the excerpt and review it another day.

Exercise 5

Music work: "Hungarian Dance No. 6" by Brahms.
Play the entire selection.

After the listeners have heard the music once, lead them in a discussion to help them recognize that Brahms alternates the bass. Part of the time he employs it to mark the accent of the syncopation or to add impetus to the vigor of the rhythm. At other times he uses it to stimulate emotional depth.
Repeat the music and review it another day.

Exercise 6

Music work: "Home to Our Mountains" from Verdi's opera *Il Trovatore.*
Play the entire selection.
Explain that the music is heard in the opera as a vocal duet between a brilliant tenor voice and a deep contralto.

Ask trainees to give special attention to the way the two voices contrast and harmonize. Request that in addition they notice the harmony of the instrumental accompaniment, especially during the interludes.
Review the music and play it on at least two other days.

Exercise 7

Music work: Roumanian Rhapsody No. 1 by Enesco.
Excerpt: begin the music at the first of the record band and continue over to where the dance-like third theme enters.
Repeat the excerpt several times and review it another day.

REACTION AWARENESS OF DYNAMICS AND VOLUME

Direct trainees to recall that people customarily increase and decrease volume in speech during any conversation. Feelings motivate speech to become louder as in anger or excitement. Soothing words are spoken more quietly and secrets are expressed in subdued tones. Establish recognition that emotions affect volume of speech.

Volume changes in musical expression are motivated by feelings and they are an important part of communication through music.

Tell trainees that you are going to play some examples of music in which volume changes contribute to the musical expression.

Ask listeners to concentrate with the aim of identifying volume contrasts and to be prepared to express opinions about the contributions made to the music meaning by these changes.

Exercise 1

Music work: "Prelude" to Verdi's opera *La Traviata.*
Play through the selection.
Present the music as a prelude to Verdi's opera, which is based on a very dramatic story. Refrain from relating the story.
Play the music.
Ask trainees what they understood from hearing the music.
Listeners usually comment first on the subdued volume of the muted strings.
They recognize that the first theme is in minor mode and the second theme in major.
Some judge the feeling expression as feelings of uneasiness, especially in the first part of the music. Others judge that it has an air of mystery and suspense.
Play the music again after the discussion.

Exercise 2

Music work: "La Garde Montante" from *Carmen Suite* by Bizet.
Play through the two bugle calls.
Play the music to the end of the second bugle call once and then inquire of the trainees what the volume indicated.
They recognize at once that the first bugle call in quiet volume suggested that it was heard from a distance and the loud volume of the second suggested it was closer to them.
Establish recognition that a composer can and does create an impression of space and distance by means of changes in volume.
Repeat the excerpt.

Exercise 3

Music work: "The Moldau" by Smetana.
Excerpt: begin at the first of the music and play through the first time the "river theme" is completed.
Before playing the music, ask students to give attention to volume changes and be ready to discuss how they contributed to the meaning and expression.
Play the excerpt once and more if requested.
Listeners will be familiar with this music from a previous

exercise. They observe at once that the volume begins quietly and increases gradually to much greater volume by the end of the completed theme. Some will interpret the meaning as suggestive of distant sounds coming closer.

Help listeners if needed to recognize that the short-tone pattern in small impulses of energy in the rhythm are representing small streams moving down the mountainside to form the source of the river. As the streams enlarge and join forces the music grows in volume. The volume continues to increase as the water expands into the great river now formed. The greatest volume comes when the full theme is introduced. It is expressive of the grandeur and power of the river.

Play the excerpt once more and review it on another day.

Exercise 4

Music work: "The Moldau" by Smetana.

Excerpt: play the final one-fourth inch of the record band, beginning just where the final motive enters, and play to the end of the music.

Explain to trainees that the motive has been called the "Vysehrad Motive." It has four grand chords. The name comes from an old castle by which the river flows. The castle has survived centuries of Czech history; once a cathedral stood within its walls. The motive is thought to resemble a religious chant in its style. It is played in massive chords by the brass, woodwind and percussion instruments.

Play the excerpt twice and ask the class what the volume expresses.

Most groups interpret it as very strong feelings of love and pride in remembering historic events connected with the old castle and that section of the Czech homeland.

Play the excerpt several times and review it another day.

Exercise 5

Music work: Fourth Movement of Beethoven's *Symphony No. 5.*

Excerpt: begin the music at the first and play through measure 25. The music is in common time.

Direct students to listen and prepare to identify the volume.

Listeners recognize the loud volume in the first hearing and usually mention the special emphasis placed right after the first beat in each of the last three measures.

All agree after discussion that the loud volume contributes greatly to the vigor and exuberance of the emotional expression in the music.

Repeat the music after discussion.

Exercise 6

Music work: "Etude in A^b" by Chopin.

Play through the selection.

Mention to the class that this etude is often called the "harp" etude. Ask the students to discover why it has been so named, while they are listening.

Develop recognition that the pianist plays the melody tones in louder volume while subduing the intricate lacework of background tones. The effect is similar to the way a design stands out on a tapestry.

Review the music on at least two other days.

Exercise 7

Music work: Fourth Movement of *Symphony No. 5* by Shostakovitch.

Present the music as an example of great contrast in volume employed to achieve the musical expression.

Ask students to identify the tone colors of the woodwind quartet.

INTRODUCING TONE TEXTURE

Present tone texture as a quality which can cause human nerves to tense or to feel soothed and comforted. There is a wide range of reaction between these two extremes which can be stimulated by tone texture.

Texture has its own special means of expression different from other components of tone quality, and from word expression. An infant in its first months of life reacts to tone texture by wincing at harsh voice sounds and being comforted and reassured by soothing sounds.

Write the words "harsh," "soothing," "dull" and "bright" on the blackboard in a position of headings. Ask students to recall sounds they have experienced which fall in each category. List the

words under the proper headings. Some which are frequently given
are:

Harsh   *Soothing*

School bells when close   Soft spoken voices
Shouting, angry voices   Chimes sounds
Shrieking automobile brakes   Breeze through tree leaves

Dull   *Bright*

Monotonous speaking voice   Ringing voice sounds
Drone of traffic sounds   Bird songs
Heavy, slow footsteps   Spontaneous laughter sounds

Mention to students that composers make frequent use of tone
texture in their musical expressions. Ask them to be especially
attentive to their own reaction to the textures in each music
example.

Exercise 1

Three music works:

"Capriccio Italien" by Tschaikowsky.
Excerpt: begin at the first of the music and play through
the bugle call section.
"Finlandia" by Sibelius.
Excerpt: begin at the first and play through the intro-
duction.
"Jesu, Joy of Man's Desiring, " by Bach.
Excerpt: begin where the brass choir enters on the
chorale theme. Play until the brass choir finishes.

Tell trainees you are presenting three kinds of trumpet tone
texture. Ask them to compare trumpet texture in each example
with those in the other two excerpts. Play each once.
Conduct a discussion to make certain that all have identified
the different textures in the three excerpts.
Play each excerpt once more.

Exercise 2

Music work: "Simple Gifts" by Copland.
Excerpt: begin the music on the second variation where the
trombone enters on the theme and the strings enter shortly after.
Ask listeners to judge which of the two tone colors has the
smoother texture—the trombone or strings.

It may be necessary to play the excerpt several times before they discover that the trombone, as played here, is smoother in texture than the strings.

Repeat the excerpt after they have reached a decision through discussion.

Exercise 3

Music work: "Intermezzo" from *Carmen Suite* by Bizet.

Play through the selection.

Direct listeners to count how many different tone textures they hear on the melody. Ask them to name the family of instruments from which the textures are heard.

Play the music twice and more if requested.

By the end of the third hearing, at most, all listeners will have become aware that there are three different woodwind textures and three string textures including the harp.

Repeat the music after discussion.

Exercise 4

Music work: "La Garde Montante" from *Carmen Suite* by Bizet.

Excerpt: begin at the first of the music and continue until the piccolo has completed the first theme twice.

Ask listeners to be especially alert to the difference in tone texture of the trumpet, piccolo and plucked string tones. Conduct a discussion to compare the three.

Play the music once more.

Exercise 5

Three music works:

"Afternoon of a Faun" by Debussy.

Excerpt: play through the opening theme in flute tone color.

"Dance of the Flutes" from *Nutcracker Suite* by Tschaikowsky.

Excerpt: begin at the first of the music and play through the theme once.

"The Moldau" by Smetana.

Excerpt: begin at the first of the music and play through measure eight. The music is in 6/8 meter.

Play each example twice.

Direct listeners to give special attention to the different tone texture · of the flute in each example as a preparation for discussion.

Repeat the music after discussion.

Exercise 6

Two music works:

"The Swan" by Saint-Saëns.

Excerpt: begin at the first of the music and play through the theme twice in 'cello tone color.

Third Movement of Beethoven's *Symphony No. 5.*

Excerpt: begin the music about one-fourth inch over on the record band, where the 'cellos and string basses begin a rapid tempo tone pattern in low range accompaniment. It is in rough texture. The sound is gruff and even ferocious.

Ask listeners to note the difference in texture between these low string sounds of the two examples.

Play the excerpts twice each.

Permit a brief discussion about the expression through texture in Saint-Saëns' music as it differs from Beethoven's in the low string tones.

Repeat each example once more.

Exercise 7

Music work: Third Movement of Mahler's *Symphony No. 1.*

Play the entire selection.

Request that listeners observe how much added contrast Mahler gains by changing texture as well as tone color.

Play the music.

Permit a short discussion about the textures observed while hearing and repeat the music once more.

Teacher A made a practice of asking students to write a paper describing two positive and two negative experiences with tone texture during one day. The papers were read in class. The assigned title was "Tone Texture in My Day."

He reported that students had fun with the expressions in the papers. They developed a significant amount of reaction awareness to tone textures through writing the assignment.

CHAPTER TEN

Presenting Obvious and Subtle Contrasts in Percussion Tone Colors, Harmony and Key Modulation

In this chapter the instructor will conclude presentation of exercises to establish reaction awareness of instrumental tone colors. He will have developed student capacity to receive direct communication through this one of the four most fundamental music elements. The achievement is one of which he can be justly proud.

Harmony exercises in section two for hearing parts sounded between identical or similar tone colors offer a strong challenge. They have proved to be a most effective means for motivating listeners to center full attention on this element of music.

Evaluation exercises in the last section are designed to lead trainees in taking the first step toward synthesizing the many listening skills they have been working to achieve heretofore.

INTRODUCING THE PERCUSSION FAMILY

A majority of trainees has been found to be familiar with the sounds of percussion instruments. They can readily identify each through hearing it.

If the teacher finds he has students unfamiliar with these sounds, it is recommended that he present the percussion section from one of the record albums entitled "Instruments of the Orchestra." There are several excellent ones available. One or two hearings of the percussion sounds will suffice to establish hearing recognition of the instruments.

The objective in these exercises is to briefly review basic percussion sounds, and then to present excerpts of music which bring recognition of communication being expressed through them. Percussions do this even though most of the instruments lack facilities for playing a melody.

Display poster-sized pictures of these percussion instruments.

Ask listeners to give attention to the sounds of each percussion instrument and to observe the expression created.

Exercise 1

Music work: Britten's "Young People's Guide to the Orchestra."

Play through variation marked M or 13.

Direct students to keep faces front and turn only their eyes toward the picture of the instrument they are hearing.

Review the music on another day.

Exercise 2

Music work: "Habañera" from *Carmen Suite* by Bizet.

Play the entire selection.

Ask students to listen especially for the communication expressed by percussion sounds and to be ready for a short discussion after they hear the music.

During the discussion, draw listeners' recognition of the zest and fiery energy created in the music by the percussion sounds.

Repeat the music after discussion.

Exercise 3

Music work: "Dance of the Sugar Plum Fairy" from *Nutcracker Suite* by Tschaikowsky.

Play through the music.

Students will be familiar with the music from hearing it in the exercise on clarinet tone color.

Request that foremost attention be given to sounds of the celesta tone color.

Play the music once and review it on another day.

Exercise 4

Music work: "Les Toréadors" from *Carmen Suite* by Bizet.
Play through the selection.

Direct students to keep alert so as to recognize every percussion sound made in the music. They are to be prepared to discuss what they hear.

During discussion, establish awareness of the excitement, pomp and grandeur created through percussion sounds.

Repeat the music after discussion.

Exercise 5

Music work: Second Movement of Beethoven's *Symphony No. 9.*

Excerpt: play the last half-inch of the record band.

Introduce this music as an example of tympani tone. It is played in a solo.

The excerpt is started before the tympani solo begins so students gain understanding of the expression before the final sounds are heard.

Repeat the music several times.

Exercise 6

Music work: "Danse Bohème" from *Carmen Suite* by Bizet.

Excerpt: play the last one-fourth inch of the record band two or three times.

Through a short discussion establish recognition that Bizet builds the wild frenzy expressed in the final measures of the music, chiefly through speeding tempo and percussion sounds.

Exercise 7

Music work: "Toccata for Percussion" by Carlos Chavez.
Play through Movement Four.

Ask students to turn their eyes toward the picture of the instrument which they hear, while keeping faces turned front.

Direct listeners to give full attention to detecting four different rhythm patterns being sounded in the music, and play the music again.

When they have heard the music once or twice, ask them to identify the rhythm patterns they have heard by clapping them for the class. Have the class as a whole clap each of the patterns.

Play the music once more.

RESPONSE TO HARMONY BETWEEN
SIMILAR TONE COLORS

Harmony parts between similar tone colors are more difficult to identify than parts between contrasting tone colors.

Exercises described in this section are designed to extend hearing identification of harmony sounds. They help develop reaction awareness of these more subtle expressions where tone colors are identical or similar.

Explain to trainees that you want them to hear and recognize each part in the harmony. They are to listen with the aim of detecting two, three or more harmony sounds which combine with the melody, and for those sounding in the background.

Exercise 1

Music work: "Capriccio Italien" by Tschaikowsky.

Excerpt: begin where "Italian Theme One" enters the first time. That is about one inch over on the record band. Play through the theme as it comes the second time.

Play the excerpt twice or more after directing students to listen for harmony parts moving with the melody.

Conduct a discussion to establish recognition that an alto part is being played in the same tone color as the melody tones.

Repeat the music once more.

Exercise 2

Music work: "Roumanian Rhapsody No. 1" by Enesco.

Excerpt: begin at the first of the music. Play through the familiar IA and IB themes and through the section where theme two is played by the strings in their upward sweep.

Conduct a discussion to make sure all are aware of the harmony parts which add so much to the expression of this music. It may be necessary to repeat the excerpt a number of times because the tone colors are often identical in the harmony parts.

Exercise 3

Music work: "Clair de Lune," orchestral version, by Debussy.

Excerpt: begin at the first of the music and play 28 measures. It is in 9/8 meter.

Play the excerpt two or three times.

Conduct a discussion to gain assurance that all listeners hear the harmony parts when the woodwinds play the theme and again when the strings play it.

Repeat the music again.

Exercise 4

Music work: First Movement of Schubert's *Unfinished Symphony.*

Excerpt: begin the music after the introduction and play through the theme twice.

Make certain, through discussion, that listeners are aware of the two parts being sounded by the violins.

Repeat the music once more.

Exercise 5

Music work: "Andante," Second Movement of Haydn's *Surprise Symphony.*

Excerpt: begin at the first of the music and play through the first variation.

Play the excerpt once.

Conduct a brief discussion to make certain that listeners recognize the examples of where harmony parts combine with melody.

Repeat the music again.

Exercise 6

Music work: "Minuet" from Mozart's *Symphony No. 39.*

Play through the movement.

Conduct a discussion for comparison of listeners' observation through hearing harmony parts.

Repeat the music again.

Exercise 7

Music work: Fourth Movement of Brahm's *Symphony No. 1.*

Excerpt: begin the music on measure 29 and play through measure 60. The meter is common time.

Play the excerpt twice.

Conduct a discussion to make certain that students recognize the French horn tone on its "call" and also the harmony parts played by the brass choir which follows.

Repeat the excerpt several times and review it on several other days.

Trainees frequently indicate, through comments, that harmony sounds express deep, significant meanings for them.

The comment of Teacher A's student was typical:

"Harmony makes you experience deep feelings which you had not ever realized you had. It makes you so clearly aware of your feelings."

INTRODUCING PIANO AND HARP

Piano and harp tones are readily identified, through hearing, by nearly every trainee; one can omit exercises, therefore, for developing identification of their tone.

The objective of the exercises is to develop reaction awareness of tone colors of each instrument in some of their very expressive roles.

Piano music named in exercises one and two have proved to be effective in achieving the objective. Few of the listeners will have heard the piano played with such singing, bell-like tone colors. Exercises for harp will extend and deepen student response to its tone colors.

Display a poster-sized picture of a concert grand piano and of a harp.

Exercise 1

Introduce the piano as a member of both the string and percussion families of instruments.

Music work: "Fantasie Impromptu" by Chopin, in piano solo version.

Play the entire selection.

Play it once on the first day and review it on another day.

Exercise 2

Music work: "Andante" from Mozart's *Concerto for Piano and Orchestra, No. 21, K 467.*

Play the whole movement.

This music is always a memorable discovery for trainees. The theme imprints itself on listeners' minds during the first hearing. An aural image of the theme and tone color seems to form instantaneously in trainees' memories. Many commented that it lingered in their thoughts for hours after they left class.

Exercise 3

Music work: "Waltz of the Flowers" from *Nutcracker Suite* by Tschaikowsky.

Excerpt: begin at the first and play through the introduction with its rippling harp tone patterns on interludes and its dazzling rendition of the cadenza.

Write the word "cadenza" on the blackboard as you explain its meaning.

Play the excerpt several times and review it on other days.

Exercise 4

Music work: "Intermezzo" from *Carmen Suite* by Bizet.
Play the whole selection.

Explain to trainees that the tones they will hear in the harp accompaniment are known as broken chord tones. They are the sounds we customarily hear played as chords with all tones being sounded at the same time. In broken chord style, tones of the chord are sounded one after the other.

Play the music twice.

Review it another day.

Exercise 5

Music work: "Afternoon of a Faun" by Debussy.

Excerpt: begin at the first of the music and play to one-half inch over on the record band, when the music comes to a point of repose.

Ask the class to concentrate on the harp tone color in the accompaniment and then on the cadenza.

Repeat the excerpt at least three times.

Review it another day.

Exercise 6

Music work: "Daphnis and Chloe, Suite No. 2" by Ravel.

Excerpt: play the first one-fourth inch of the record band.

Before playing the music, mention that it has a special effect made by the harp tones. Allow listeners to discover that they are hearing many harps to make the effect.

Conduct a discussion after they listen to the music once to draw out observations on their hearing. Students often judge the sound of the harp here as similar to that made by tree leaves dancing in a lively breeze.

Repeat the excerpt several times.

Review it another day.

Exercise 7

Music work: "The Moldau" by Smetana.

Excerpt: begin the music right after the peasant wedding dance ends, and continue until the trumpet enters softly on a rhythm pattern in martial style.

Ask trainees to listen for the sounds of the harp playing the accompaniment and to prepare to suggest what the sounds represent. Play the music.

Students often suggest that the harp tones resemble those of splashing water.

Repeat the excerpt and review it on other days.

Teacher A always arranged to introduce the exercises for piano and harp during the time when students were having test week in other classes. His reason was that the music brought such rapid and deep response that the exercises were regarded as recreation activities rather than studies.

He had a second and very important objective in this habitual timing of the presentations. It was to lead students to discover, through first hand experience, the refreshing and revitalizing effect music exerted on tired minds.

EXCERPTS TO DEVELOP HEARING IDENTIFICATION OF KEY MODULATION

The objective in presenting the exercises on hearing key modulation is to develop reaction awareness of change in key. Its effect is somewhat magical. One moment the listener is feeling a strong interest in hearing the music sounds move around and toward the key name tone of one key. He hears a sound which seems foreign to the present key and suddenly he becomes aware of feeling a strong interest in urging the music toward a different name tone, to a new key.

Remind students that composers choose one key as most suitable for their expression and change to other keys when the expression demands that they do so. They also change the key to gain variety when they are repeating themes and other tone patterns.

Continue on to explain that a listener cannot in most instances accept an abrupt change from one key to another. It makes him feel confused and disoriented. The change must be made with regard for certain adjustments in the harmony which create the modulation in acceptable form.

Tell trainees you are going to present some examples of modulation for their hearing experience. You feel that it is important for them to become sensitive to key changes in order for them to fully understand the composer's expression.

Add that as a rule simple folk music, composed songs, popular and standard songs have several modulations. Music works of greater length have many modulations.

Direct listeners to make sensitive observance of how modulation in the music affects their own feeling response while they are hearing the keys changing.

Exercise 1

Music work: the song "Flow Gently Sweet Afton" by Spilman, in a four-part harmony version.

Excerpt: begin at the first of the music. Play it on the piano through the music of the words "green braes."

Play the excerpt once. Stop briefly and then sound the first tone of the key in which you are playing the song. Sound it in octaves. For instance, if the key is A^b major, play A^b in octaves.

Ask students if it sounds like the key name of the music heard in the song or if it seems to clash with that music.

Students will readily state that it sounds like the key note of the song music.

Now continue on with the song through the music of the words "thy praise," which come four measures later. Stop briefly and then sound the octaves on the A^b or key name note again.

Ask if it still sounds like the key name note.

Students will tell you at once that the sound you are playing does not belong as key note to the key they have heard in the latter measures of the song.

Repeat the second example. Stop briefly and then sound the octave of E^b or the fifth of whichever key the music started in.

Ask students if it sounds right and could be the key note of the new key. They will assert that it is.

Point out to trainees that the key shift or modulation was

signalled when a tone sounded which obviously did not belong in the first key.

Ask students to listen to the music again through the second example and to raise hands when they hear the odd tone sound.

When you play the music, hands will go up on the word "thy" before "praise."

Ask students to listen to the second example once more and to hear the chord with the odd tone resolve to a rest chord. That rest chord is the key name chord of the new key.

Play from the first of the music through the modulation several times so that listeners will hear and be aware of their feeling response to the sounds which modulate into the second key.

Exercise 2

Music work: the song "Deck The Halls," old Welsh folk song.

Excerpt: begin at the first and play through twelve measures. Play it on the piano in four-part harmony.

Write the word "modulation" on the blackboard. Ask students to keep faces front, but to turn their eyes toward the word on the board when they hear the first tone which sounds as if it does not belong to the key in which the music began.

They will hear this odd tone on the first beat of measure eleven. Play on through measure twelve.

Stop briefly and then sound the octave of the key note in which you began the song.

Establish recognition that the octave sounds do not belong as key note any longer.

Repeat the example. Pause briefly and then sound octaves of the fifth tone of the original key. Students will identify this as the key note of the new key into which the music has modulated.

Continue on and play the final four measures of the song. After a brief pause, sound the octave of the original key note heard at the opening of the song. Ask them if it sounds like the key note of the last four measures. They will agree that it does. Establish the fact that the music returned to the original key for the last four measures.

Play the song through twice more while they listen for the modulations.

Exercise 3

Music work: the song "When Johnny Comes Marching Home" by Lambert.

Excerpt: begin at the first and play through eight measures in four-part harmony. Play it on the piano.

Ask listeners to turn their eyes to the word "modulation" on the blackboard when they hear the music begin to change key.

By the time the excerpt has been heard twice most students recognize that the key modulates from minor to major on the "Hurrah, hurrah!" each time. After that the music returns to the relative minor key.

Play the excerpt several more times.

Exercise 4

Music work: "Träumerei" by Schumann.

Excerpt: play a recording of the entire selection.

Direct students to indicate each time they hear the key change by turning only their eyes toward the word "modulation" on the board.

It may be necessary to repeat the music a number of times before students identify the modulations. When they do, write the pattern on the board as they identify it as follows:

Theme of four measures stays in the first key until it has been played four times.

It modulates into another key.

It stays in the new key for eight measures and then modulates back to the first key.

Repeat the music once more.

Exercise 5

Music work: "Triumphal March" from the opera *Aida* by Verdi, recorded instrumental version.

Excerpt: begin the music on the Grand March at the close of the Thanksgiving Hymn.

Tell the students there will be key modulations and ask them to turn their eyes toward that word on the board when they hear the key change.

Listeners recognize the change to a higher key and a return to the original key with few repetitions. The modulation takes place abruptly and is done more simply. than that in "Träumerei."

Repeat the music after identification of modulations has been made.

EXPANDING COMPLEXITY OF
EVALUATION PROCEDURES

Exercises in this section are designed as a challenge to make listeners consciously search out the meter, tempo and theme beginning with the first sound of the music they hear. Trainees derive great satisfaction and self-assurance from the experience. They discover they are capable of meeting the challenge.

Explain to the class that you are going to play excerpts of music from which you want them to identify in writing the following sounds of elements:

Meter: number of beats in a measure.
Tempo: walking, running, etc.
Theme pattern: first, second, etc.
Tone color: heard on themes each time.

Add that they will be graded on accuracy and on the number of repetitions they require. After you play the excerpt twice, ask if any have completed their answers and wish to hand in their papers. Do this after each repetition, taking care to write the number of hearings on the papers as you accept them.

Exercise 1

Music work: Third Movement of Dvorak's *New World Symphony.*

Excerpt: begin at the first of the music with its tone pattern moving in octaves accompanied by a triangle rhythm pattern. Play through the first theme by oboe and flute two times, the interlude from strings and other instruments, and the third and fourth playing of the same theme on strings. Continue until a place of repose is reached by the descending brass tones in the background.

Mention to listeners that the theme is only four measures long.
Arrange for writing materials.
Play the music.
Average trainees will probably answer with somewhat the following description:

Meter: three beats in a measure.
Tempo: animated, running speed.
Theme: one, one, interlude and one, one.
Tone color on theme: woodwind twice and strings twice.

Some students will add that there was a running rhythm pattern in the background as well as a swirling motion by the strings.

Others may mention the descending tone pattern by the brasses, sounded back of the last two repetitions of the theme.

Exercise 2

Music work: Third Movement of Beethoven's *Symphony No. 6.*

Excerpt: begin at the first of the music. Play through the IA and IB themes, which are played four successive times. Continue through theme two twice, and on through the jubilant horn interlude until it is completed.

Mention to students that the first theme is sixteen measures long and had best be written as IA and IB.

Average trainees will probably answer:

Meter: three beats to a measure.

Tempo: brisk running speed.

Themes pattern: first theme four times and then second theme twice.

Tone colors: strings, woodwind and then the whole orchestra.

Some listeners will comment on the horn tone pattern presented after the second theme. Others will mention the vigorous bass tone heard on the primary accent of each measure.

Instructors have come to regard the type of exercise presented above as very important. Some select an excerpt to present, with the same objective and procedure, once a week for four to six weeks longer. They judge that it establishes a habit in trainees of actively listening and paying attention to the whole content of sounds as the listener must do to gain communication. The exercises prevent students from falling back into a passive attitude toward listening.

CHAPTER ELEVEN

Identifying Voice Tone Colors Through Hearing Sense Alone

Presentations described in this chapter provide an instructor with means for guiding listeners to one of the most significant discoveries in all of music expression. That is reaction awareness of beautiful, enlivening, musical tone color from the world's most choice singing voices. They are one of the natural resources of humanity. These voices belong to the people more than to the individuals of whom they are a part. They create feelings of well-being, wonder, inspiration and enlightenment in all who hear them well enough to react to them with awareness.

Our objective in presenting the voices is to develop listeners' ability to identify each type of voice tone color through hearing and to make trainees instantly aware of their own personal reaction to those tones.

Some of our early experiments included operatic arias, personal favorites, which proved too dramatic for our exercises. Arias of intense emotional expression are sometimes overwhelming before they have been heard and seen in their true context in the opera. There the plot, dramatic action and other aspects of expression build the listener's response up to the emotional level for accepting such high emotional intensity. When the arias are heard in concert without the aids present in opera performance, the listener is unable to accept them as credible. Two examples of those we found were "Vesti la Giubba" from *Pagliacci* by Leonacavallo, and the famed "Quartet" from Act IV of *Rigoletto* by Verdi. Trainees often found the sobbing sounds in Leoncavallo's song suspect, sometimes even comical. They found the complexity of sounds in Verdi's "Quartet" something of a confusion of competing sounds.

Selections which are suggested in the exercises are ones which did not prove dependent upon the opera. They present the voice colors in a manner very suitable for reaching our objective.

Each instructor must decide whether his equipment and recordings can produce the women's voice sounds authentically. Their tones can be easily distorted. If they are, it is better to omit the exercises for soprano and contralto voices.

Another problem which may appear is the one of balance of volume with the area of the music room. If the volume must be turned up to be suitable for the area of a concert hall in order to get authentic tone color of voice, it is better not to present the exercises, or to present them in an assembly hall, if available. These matters are of first importance. If we desregard them we develop a lasting, negative response to vocal music literature. When the voice sounds are authentic, the experiences with the exercises are a delight to trainees and to their teachers.

It is possible to bring listeners voice sounds of the most beautiful singing voices past and present. Recordings should be selected from them.

Explain to students that you are going to present examples of various types of men's and women's voices. You want them to listen with special attention given to tone color of each type as it differs from the other types. Upon completing the exercises you will expect them to identify voice types through hearing alone.

COMPARING TONE COLOR AND TEXTURE OF TENOR AND BARITONE VOICES

Explain to trainees that the tenor voice tones sound in a higher range of pitch than those of the baritone voice, but that the tone color differences are the ones you want them to identify and remember. Mention that hearing reactions to the tone color and texture of one type of voice will differ from those to another type. You want them to form an aural image of each while listening.

Exercise 1

Music work: "La Mattinata" by Leoncavallo, in tenor voice recording.

Play the whole song.

Teach the class to sing an English translation of the song. The key will need to be lower than tenor range.

Present the recording as an example of tenor voice tone color.

Play the music at least three times on different days. The song is excellent for demonstrating the brilliance and buoyancy of the tenor voice.

Before the third hearing, direct trainees to take note of the way in which the composer contrasts and then supports the voice through his accompaniment.

Exercise 2

Music work: "O Sole Mio" by di Capau, in tenor voice recording.

Play all the song.

Teach the class to sing the song in English.

Present the music as an example of tenor voice tone quality. Play it twice on different days.

This song rapidly forms an aural image for listeners.

Exercise 3

Music work: "Di Provenza il mar" (Thy Home in Fair Provence) from Verdi's opera *La Traviata.*

Play the whole song.

Teach the class to sing an English version of the song. It is not advisable to relate the whole story of the opera. Merely explain the situation as it exists in the opera at this meeting of father and son.

The son has broken with his family over his romance with a woman they cannot accept. He has left home. The father strives to heal the breach and to persuade his son to return to their home with him. The father reminds him of their former happy times and existence at Provence.

Present the music as an example of baritone voice tones.

Play the music at least twice on different days with listeners concentrating on tone color. Call attention to Verdi's accompaniment before the third hearing.

The instrumental tone colors are in the same low range as the voice. They are as close to tone color of the voice as any instruments can be. Verdi evidently intended to make the contrast between voice texture and string texture.

Harmony parts should be recognized and so, too, should the way Verdi employs the woodwinds in higher range harmony parts, on interludes and in the background. They are complimentary to the dark velvet-like tone of the voice and the strings.

Call student attention to the way the string rhythm serves to keep the right sense of needed motion.

Exercise 4

Music work: "The Sun Worshippers," a tribal ritual song of the Zuni Indians. Recorded by baritone voice.

Play the complete song.

Present the recording as an example of baritone voice tone.

Explain that the song was created as part of a ceremonial in worship of the sun. Before dawn the Sun-Priest summons his people to greet the sun. When they are gathered he offers a prayer for aid and guidance as the sun appears. Play the song on two different days.

Exercise 5

Music work: "Ah! Mimi, Tu piu" (Ah! Mimi, Thou False One) from Puccini's opera *La Bohème.*

Play the whole song.

Present the music as a duet between two leading characters, one a tenor and the other a baritone.

Explain that the two young men, both students of the arts in Paris, are seen at work in a large attic room. Both have been deserted by their sweethearts for more affluent suitors.

One is attempting to paint and the other to write. Up to this time they have each avoided speaking about the girls, but one picks up some ribbon left by one girl and they begin to talk in song about their feelings concerning Mimi and Musetta.

Play the song on two different days and ask listeners to pay special attention to the contrast in tone color and texture between the two types of voices.

INTRODUCING BASS AND COLORATURA SOPRANO

Tell students you are going to present the highest and lowest range voice types in contrast with each other.

Ask trainees to listen with the aim of developing an aural image of each type of voice, and to give special attention to their own reaction to each tone color.

Exercise 1

Music work: "La Vergine degli angeli" (May Angels Guard Thee) from Verdi's opera *Forza del Destino.*
Play through the song.
Explain to trainees that the song is heard during a church scene. The music is sung as a duet between Leonora, a leading character of soprano voice, and the Abbot of bass voice. She is receiving a prayerful blessing from him.
Play the music on two different days.

Exercise 2

Music work: "Coronation Scene" from Moussorgsky's opera *Boris Godounow.*
Play the whole song.
Introduce the music as one of the greatest songs in music literature for the basso voice.
Tell the class that there is a crowd of people waiting before the Red Stairway leading from the Czar's apartments. They are waiting for their new Czar, Boris, to appear.
When he comes, he. sings a solo in which he asks divine guidance in facing responsibilities of ruling the nation.
Play the music on two separate days.

Exercise 3

Music work: "Caro Nome" (Dearest Name) from Verdi's opera *Rigoletto,* with orchestral accompaniment.
Play through the selection.
Introduce the aria as an example of coloratura soprano tone color which is in the highest range of any human voice.
This is one of the most beloved arias in all of opera literature.
Explain that the leading lady, Gelda, is singing of her love in words to the effect that his name is carved forever upon her heart.
Ask students to center attention on voice tone color and on its amazing agility as it vies with the flute.
When trainees become more familiar with the music, conduct a short discussion to establish awareness of the instrumental accompaniment and its beautiful contributions to the musical expression.

Review the music after discussion.

Exercise 4

Music work: "Alleluia" from Mozart's motet *Exsultate jubilate* (exult, rejoice).

Play the whole song.

Introduce the music as another great favorite for coloratura soprano voice. This is an example of Mozart's style at its very best.

After the students have heard the excerpt once or twice, ask them to give special attention to the effect which primary accents add to the expression of delicate grace, and yet of positive, animated motion.

Review this music at times when students' mental processes appear to need revitalization.

IDENTIFYING SOPRANO AND CONTRALTO TONE COLORS

Explain that the soprano voice to be heard in the next exercises is not as high in range as the coloratura and its tone color will be different. The contralto voice is the lowest one in women's voice range. Its tone color differs greatly from the soprano's.

Ask trainees to listen with the aim of forming an aural image of each voice type.

Exercise 1

Music work: "Musetta Waltz" from Puccini's opera *La Bohème.*

Play the whole song.

Introduce the music as an example of soprano tone color.

Teach the class to sing an English translation of the song.

Explain that the setting of the scene is in a restaurant on Christmas Eve. Musetta, a young girl soprano, enters with an elderly banker as her escort. She is dressed elegantly. She selects a table next to a group of young people, one of whom is her lover, Marcel. They have had a quarrel. In singing the song she hopes to lose the aged banker and depart with Marcel.

Play the music several times on different days.

Exercise 2

Music work: "Ai Nostri Monti" (Home to Our Mountains) from Verdi's opera *Il Trovatore.*

Play through the whole song.

Introduce the music as an example of contralto tone color, contrasted with tenor in a duet.

Teach the class to sing an English translation of the song, with male voices singing Manrico's part and female voices singing Azucena's.

Explain that the duet is sung by two leading characters who are prisoners sentenced to death. Manrico sings to his Gypsy mother in an attempt to calm her fears. He reminds her of their home in the mountains where he assures her they will soon return. Azucena becomes comforted by his song and joins in the singing.

Play the music and center attention on the voice tone colors until they are familiar. After that direct attention to the wonderfully expressive sounds of the accompaniment.

Play the music once more.

Exercise 3

Music work: "He Shall Feed His Flock" from Handel's oratorio *The Messiah.*

Play through the song.

Mention that the song was originally intended for soprano voice. After consideration Handel changed it into the deeper, richer tones of the contralto voice.

Play the music several times on different days.

Teacher A had a more than ample record budget. He often presented recordings of two different singers of the same voice type on the same music work. He would ask listeners to compare the expression of the two artists. He judged that listener awareness was broadened greatly by this practice. For instance, in the tenor voice selections, he would present Tagliavini's and Bjoerling's recording or Bjoerling's and Tucker's recording of the same selection.

EVALUATING VOICE IDENTIFICATION PROGRESS BY TONE COLORS FROM A CHORAL WORK

Exercise 1

Music work: "Hallelujah Chorus" from Handel's oratorio *The Messiah.*

Play through the selection.

Explain to listeners that you are going to present choral music in which the voices sometimes move chordwise in four-part harmony similar to the style of a hymn. At other times one type of voice will carry the melody while the rest of the voices produce background effects in tone and ryhthm patterns with harmony.

Direct them to write down which type of voice sings the theme each time it is heard. They are to watch for a signal from you to indicate when they are to begin writing. Add that you will also signal when they are to cease writing. There will be two different sections where they are to write.

Arrange for writing materials.

Begin the music at the first. The meter is common time. Signal trainees to begin writing on measure 17 and to cease with measure 32.

In measure 17 the contralto voice takes the melody singing the following words: "For the Lord God Omnipotent reigneth."

The same theme and words pass to each of the following voices:

Soprano, tenor and contralto again.

Continue on with the music. Signal listeners to write again on measure 41 and to cease with measure 52.

In this section the bass voices will take the melody on the words: "And He shall reign forever and ever."

The theme will pass from bass to each of the following tone colors:

Tenor, contralto and soprano.

Play the music to its conclusion.

Repeat if requested.

Exchange papers, check and record grades.

Repeat the music while students have their corrected papers before them.

Review it another day.

EXTENDING EXPERIENCES WITH VOICE TONES IN COMBINATION AND CONTRAST

Exercise 1

Music work: "Send Out Thy Light" by Charles Gounod. Present a recorded version by one of the éxcellent choral groups. Play the whole song.

Our objective is to give further experience to trainees in hearing voice tone colors in harmony while becoming familiar with an enduring choral favorite.

Write the English translation words on the blackboard. Have the class practice reading the words aloud in choric speech. Try to achieve genuine, meaningful expression.

Tell the class you want it to listen to the song one time and then try to hum its melody by memory. Play the music more than once, if necessary, for the students to remember and hum it.

Play the music once more and request them to listen especially for harmony parts and tone colors.

Repeat the music after a few days.

Exercise 2

Music work: "Libiamo ne lieti calici" (Let Us Drink from Festive Cups) from Verdi's opera *La Traviata.*

Play all of the selection.

Our objective is to increase experience of listeners in hearing voice tone colors and instrumental tone colors combined and contrasted. At the same time they become familiar with this joyous music.

Explain that the music is the opening number of the opera. The leading man, Alfredo, sings a toast at the request of the leading lady, Violetta. They are with a large group of friends at a banquet.

The toast is to wine, love, beauty and joy of living. At intervals chorus voices join the tenor soloist. Violetta then takes up the melody and finally all join in the singing.

Direct listeners to notice the voice contrasts between the two solo voices in both color and texture. Note the way Violetta's tones resonate and resound against the deeper male voice tones of the chorus in the last part of the music.

Ask the class to hum the melody after they hear the music. They will respond with zest and with ease.

On another day play the music for them to listen again, and to move their toes in a waltz step to the rhythm while they remain seated.

Exercise 3

Music work: "Pilgrims' Chorus" from Wagner's opera *Tannhäuser.* Choose a recording by an excellent choral group. Play the whole song.

Our objective is to broaden listener experience with great choral music literature and to concentrate attention on voice contrasts in very unusual harmonic progressions.

Tell students to especially notice the modulations and the harmonies.

Write an English translation of the words on the blackboard for students to study for a short time before they listen to the music.

Mention that the great chorus of pilgrims has completed a journey of penitence to Rome. They are returning joyfully to their native land. Listeners are to be prepared to hum the melody after they hear it.

Review the music another day.

Teachers in general have expressed surprise at the deep impression voice tone color exercises have made on trainees. Since experience with voice tones begins in early life and continues daily in speech and often in singing, instructors had felt that they were reviewing rather than presenting new experiences.

A factor which had gone unrecognized was that few listeners would have heard any one of the world's most choice singing voices performing music on the level of their understanding. Had these listeners heard one of these voices singing a familiar song such as "Shenandoah" or "Down in the Valley" they would have developed instant reaction awareness of the wonderful tone color.

There are few opportunities to hear the most gifted voices live or on recordings in simple familiar songs. These voices are to be heard mostly in concert and operatic music. This music is often not at all meaningful to the unskilled listener and so countless individuals are never aware that these superb voices exist.

Our trainees have become skilled listeners by the time we present the voice tone color exercises. They have become capable of understanding the expression of the music while gaining reaction awareness of the musical sounds of these great voices.

The enthusiasm and delight expressed in trainee response comes about by the above developments.

CHAPTER TWELVE

Recognizing Design and Form Through Hearing

In former chapters listening trainees and instructors have been involved with four music elements which express the content of meaning and emotion created in the music. In the present chapter attention will be directed toward a fifth element, form or design, which makes a different contribution. It does not serve as a means of direct communication from composer to listener through the hearing reaction to sound. It serves to make a pattern of order through which the expression projects to the listener.

The objective in giving exercises for form identification is to develop recognition of basic conventional form structures in music on the level of present trainee understanding. This seems to develop skill and readiness to understand larger and more complex forms as the trainee increases his familiarity with music literature.

IDENTIFYING FORM AFTER LISTENERS ARE FAMILIAR WITH A MUSIC WORK

Explain to the class that form or design in music evolved during composers' search for impressive patterns in which to express their musical meanings and emotions. Their first problem was to catch the interest of listeners with a theme as the subject. Next came a concern for retaining interest in the music which followed ·

Composers were greatly influenced through discovery of certain tendencies in human nature. Observation of these tendencies has led to formulation of what is sometimes called laws of expression in the arts. They tell us that essentials of acceptable expression are:

> Variety and contrast,
> Repetition for unity, and
> Balance between repetition and contrast.

Repetition is necessary to create a semblance of unity. Too much repetition creates boredom and results in loss of interest. Variety and contrast serve to renew and retain interest, but when used to extreme they overwhelm the listeners and replace interest with confusion. Balance is necessary.

In addition, consideration of these laws taught the composer that his theme must catch the initial interest of a listener. He saw that two or more themes were needed for contrast. He learned to repeat the themes in a work of any length in order to attain unity and create a lasting impression. When and if he overused repetition the listener's interest would be withdrawn. If contrast was employed to excess the listener became over stimulated, confused and finally withdrew attention.

Add that not all music is created within a definite pattern or design. We can separate music into two great classes, "Program Music" and "Absolute Music." The former is written without concern for conventional forms, while the latter is written with careful regard. Much of the world's great and enduring music literature falls in the latter classification.

In order to make certain that trainees are impressed with the strength and depth of human reactions implied in the "laws of art," conduct a question-and-answer check.

To demonstrate effects of excessive repetition:

Ask a student to name his favorite food. When he answers, ask how he imagines he would react to eating it for every meal over a week's time.

Ask a trainee to name his favorite color. Inquire what his

reaction would probably be to an imaginary room with walls, ceiling, floor and furniture all in that color.

For accentuating the effect of too much contrast:

Ask a listener how he would react to having the furniture in his living quarters moved all around each day.

Ask students to imagine their reaction to school days where a different time, class schedule and duration of class were announced each day.

Tell listeners you are going to begin the exercises by identifying the forms of music with which they are familiar.

Exercise 1

Three music works:

"Old Smoky"—American folk song.
"Down in the Valley"—American folk song.
"Traumerei" by Robert Schumann.

Play each selection on the piano or by a recording. Lead listeners to discover that each has only one theme.
Tell students each example is in one-part form.

Exercise 2

Four music works:

"America" by Henry Carey.
"Londonderry Air," an Irish folk song.
"L'il 'Liza Jane," Negro folk song.
"Over the Meadow," Czech folk song.

Play each selection and guide listeners to recognize that there are two themes in each.
Arrange for writing materials.
Ask trainees to write the theme pattern of each as they listen. Students will easily detect the following patterns:

"America"—A, B.
"Londonderry Air"—A, A, B, B.
"L'il 'Liza Jane"—A, A, B, B.
"Over the Meadow"—A, A, B, B.

Explain that this form is called binary or two-part form. It is found in many folk songs.

Exercise 3

Three music works:

"All Through the Night," old Welsh song.
"Bonnie Doon," Scotch folk song.
"The Minstrel Boy," old Irish air.

Play each song and ask students to write the theme patterns, which are:

"All Through the Night"—A, A, B, A.
"Bonnie Doon"—A, A, B, A.
"The Minstrel Boy"—A, A, B, A.

Explain that the pattern is called ternary or three-part form.

REVIEWING SELECTIONS FOR FORM IDENTIFICATION

Ask trainees to listen and classify selections in the exercises as one of the following forms: one-part, binary or ternary.

Exchange papers, check and record grades from the exercises.

Exercise 1

Music work: "Wedding Day at Troldhaugen" by Grieg.
Play through the selection.

Repeat, if requested, in order for the trainees to recognize the three-part or ternary form.

Exercise 2

Music work: "Lullaby" by Brahms.
Play through the music which is in two-part or binary form.
Repeat if requested.

Exercise 3

Music work: "Minuet" from Mozart's *G Minor Symphony* which is in three sections, making it ternary form. Play the entire movement.

Repeat once for students to check on their answers. Play more if requested.

PRESENTING CONVENTIONAL FORMS

Explain to trainees that the majority of shorter music works is written in one of three forms which they have been identifying in the exercises just completed.

Introduce the rondo form as a fourth pattern which has been popular with composers for generations.

It is thought that rondo form developed from a type of old European singing game. The entire group of players would dance around in a circle singing a simple tune. When it was completed, all stopped and one member of the group was given the nod to sing a tune of his own creation. If he did not accept the challenge, he paid a forfeit and another player was challenged.

When the newly created tune was completed, the group would dance around and sing the first tune once more. The possibilities for contrast were more than generous.

The rondo form developed with composers as an "A" theme contrasting with a "B" theme, a "C" theme and sometimes even a "D" theme.

The part sung by the whole group was called "rondeau" by the French and "round" by the English. Gradually the form came to be known as "rondo."

Exercise 1

Music work: Second Movement, "Andante," from *Eine Kleine Nachtmusic* (Serenade for Strings) K 525, by Mozart.

Play through the movement.

Introduce the music as an example of rondo form.

Direct students to listen to the music once before they try to write down the letter pattern of themes. Warn them that there are some tone patterns which are not themes, but are introduced to serve as connecting links between themes.

The pattern of themes is A-B-A-C-A, followed by a short coda. Each theme is repeated at least once each time and the "A" and "C" themes more than once.

Exchange papers, check and record grades.

Repeat the music while the checked papers are before the students.

Exercise 2

Music work: "Cattle Blues" (Plow that Broke the Plains) by Virgil Thomson.

Play the whole selection

Introduce the music as an example of rondo form.

Explain to trainees that the themes are taken from American cowboy songs.

Ask listeners to hear the music once and then to write the theme pattern while hearing it the second time.

The pattern of themes is A-B-A-C-A-B-A-C.

Repeat as requested.

Exchange papers, check and record grades.

Exercise 3

Music work: Second Movement from Haydn's *Surprise Symphony.*

Introduce the music as an example of "Theme and Variation" form.

Listeners will be familiar with the themes "A" and "B" from a previous exercise.

Play the music once on several different days.

Exercise 4

Music work: "Simple Gifts" from *Appalachian Spring* by Copland.

Play the whole selection.

Introduce it for review. Mention that it is an example of "Theme and Variations" form

Play it at least twice.

INTRODUCING SONATA FORM

In early experiments it was discovered that students, when given the outline of sonata form to observe before hearing it, became so intent on following the outline that they gave little attention to the whole expression of the music. Sounds of other elements, except melody, were excluded. For this reason the exercises are designed so the listener will discover the pattern of form while first listening to sounds of all the elements in the music. Then he is given an outline of the form.

The objective in the exercises is to first lead trainees to identify and become familiar with each of the themes through hearing, and then to guide them to gradual recognition of the design of sonata form. They hear the pattern in which the themes succeed each other. They hear the variety of ways contrast is created in themes, rhythms, etc.

It. is relatively easy to teach the class to sing several of the

German folk songs which have a hint in their expression of the characteristics we find in Beethoven's music. There is a gusto and humor combined with feelings of well-being. The following songs are suggested:

"German Peasants' Dance," a Wurttemberg folk song.

"Kathryn's Wedding Day," a German tune.

"Holla Hi, Holla Ho!," a Bavarian folk song.

"Now Show Me Your Foot," a German folk song which students enjoy in a folk-dance-and-pantomime combination.

Exercise 1

Music work: First Movement of Beethoven's *Symphony No. 8.*

Excerpt: begin the music at the first and play through the exposition of the four themes. Later play through the whole movement.

Introduce the music as an example of sonata form. Explain that many of the larger music works are written in this form, because it provides for repetition and contrast while preserving unity.

Tell trainees you are going to play the first theme for them to learn. They may write a dash pattern or just listen. They will be expected to hum the theme when they have heard it three or four times.

The music begins with the first sound of theme one. It is in 3/4 meter.

Play through the theme. The first half is in string tone and the second half in woodwind tone. Then the second half is repeated in string tone. Play it two or three times and then ask listeners to hum it. Insist that they hum it with the same expressive gusto and vibrancy as they heard from the recording.

As soon as they can hum it correctly, play the theme again for them to identify tone colors.

Exercise 2

Direct students to be prepared to follow the same procedure with theme two as they did in Exercise 1. The theme begins with the very next note after theme one is concluded.

Warn students that the bass part has a vigor and attention-getting rumble which may divert them from recognizing the theme played in higher strings.

Play the music from the first through theme two, its repetition, and the extension made by repeating a short pattern of the last few notes. Repeat it twice and then call for trainees to hum theme two. Repeat again if necessary.

When they are sure of theme two, ask them to sing theme one and then theme two.

Exercise 3

Explain that theme three enters with graceful motion in string tone at the end of theme two. Ask them to prepare to hear it several times and learn it as they did the first two themes. Again they will be asked to hum it after several hearings.

Play through theme three on strings and then its repetition on the woodwinds several times. Call attention to the ritards in the tempo at the end of the theme both times it is played.

After they learn it, ask them to identify the tone color in which the theme was played.

Play from the first of the music through two renditions of theme three.

Exercise 4

Tell the class you are now going to play through an interlude between themes three and four, which serves as a connecting bridge. Play it several times and encourage recognition that it is a sprightly tone pattern of string tone above zestful bass support.

Lead listeners to notice how, as the music crescendos, the basses gradually create a pompous style in preparation for the entrance of theme four. The music reaches a climax.

Exercise 5

Instruct listeners to prepare to identify and learn theme four well enough to hum it. It follows immediately after the build-up of tone and volume.

When they have heard it once, draw attention to the gruff, vigorous rhythm motion of the first half of theme four, as it contrasts with the smooth grace of the last half.

Students have described the first half of theme four as being "suggestive of a bear skipping on his hind feet."

Make listeners aware of string tone color on the first half of the theme and woodwinds taking over the last half of the theme.

When all have learned to hum theme four, have the low voices of the class hum the first half and mark the bass rhythm on their desks with the palms of their hands. Have the high voices hum the second half while they do a waltz step on the desks with their fingers substituting for feet.

Exercise 6

Explain to trainees that the opening section in which each theme was introduced is called the "Exposition" section of sonata form. Themes are presented as the chief subjects of the music expression to come.

The next section which they are to hear shortly will present the four themes with many changes in rhythm patterns, keys, tone colors, etc. The sounds will express many aspects of the meaning contained in the themes. A composer's imagination and creative resources are tested to the extreme in the second section, which has come to be known as the "Development" section of sonata form.

The third section presents the themes in a final restatement. It is called the "Recapitulation" section. This movement of Beethoven's has a coda, or passage, added to give a feeling of finality and close to the music.

Tell trainees that you are going to start the music at the first of the movement and play through all three sections and coda.

Remind listeners that the composer's expression projects to them through rhythm, melody, tone color and harmony while sounded in the pattern of form. You feel full confidence in their skill for hearing the whole expression with understanding and awareness.

Tell them they will, no doubt, find that they add to what they hear each time for the first half-dozen hearings. That is true with the majority of even skillful listeners.

Play the music.

Review it several times over the next few weeks. It will gain favor with each repetition.

Summarize on the blackboard:

Sonata Form:

Exposition
Development
Recapitulation

Teacher A happened onto an interesting experience which revealed student response to the exercises above.

He went to see the physical education teacher about school business for a moment between classes. That teacher was working in the auditorium on a program rehearsal. As Teacher A entered the back stage area, he came upon a group of students passing time waiting for their teacher to come in.

They were merrily singing the first theme of Beethoven's music on neutral syllables something like "ta-da," while they executed a vigorous dance step in a circle. He judged this one of the clearest proofs of the creation of an aural image in the listeners.

Teacher B had a father approach him at a P.T.A. meeting with the following remark:

"I rarely make it to a P.T.A. meeting, but I had to come tonight. I had to meet the teacher who could bring our Mike to spend his own money on a classical music record. He is usually so tight with his money!"

The boy was a fifteen-year-old student who had not expressed more than average interest in the symphony music of Beethoven, but who had found it meaningful enough to part with his own money to obtain the record.

Most students will not recognize for some time that they have undergone a change of great importance while involved with the exercises on sonata form. It will be months and perhaps even a year or two after they leave class before most will observe that during these exercises they changed the image they held of Beethoven. He had been vaguely regarded as a famous composer of complex classical music; he was now a composer of meaningful and interesting expression which came well within their understanding.

CHAPTER THIRTEEN

Establishing Habitual Procedures for First Listening Study of a Music Work

A change of procedure appears in this chapter and in those to follow. It is made to prepare trainees for independent listening study of music literature. Students will gain understanding without need for guidance or direction of others.

During training exercises the student has depended upon the teacher to direct his attention to specific sounds. He has been motivated to pay attention by knowing that evaluation exercises would measure his responses. Listeners are now skilled enough to hear the whole content of sounds in a music work without teacher help. Most will be unaware of this ability until led in actual experiences which demonstrate their skill.

A second objective is to develop a formula through class discussion. It is to be for use in learning to understand a music work which is unknown to the listener. Repeated use of this formula in class, during the exercises to understand whole music works, will establish habitual use by the trainee. It will lead him to independence in hearing and learning to understand other music selections of his choice.

Students will already have a partial understanding of a number of music works. Involvement with exercises from previous chapters will have brought them to identify and become familiar with themes of more than sixty-five choice works of music literature. When themes are familiar to a listener, he is well on the way toward understanding what the music expresses.

Many students will have acquired and listened to recordings of selections from which they have heard excerpts in class. They will be much more adept at hearing full content of the music than those who have heard only excerpts.

Presentations for a variety of music selections are provided in order that the teacher may choose those he thinks are more appropriate for a given class. With some groups he may wish to present all of them. The selections were chosen from many employed in experiments. They were demonstrated to be within the range of listening skill of average trainees, and proved effective for gaining the objectives.

Conduct the discussion with the class to create a formula or workable pattern of procedure for going about learning a music work new to students. As the plan is formulated, write it on the blackboard and have students make a copy of it. The following steps should evolve from the discussion:

1. Listen, with the beginning of the first measure, to detect rhythm meter and tempo, so that you may feel and identify with the motion and speed of the music.
2. Be alert to adjust your feeling and perception of motion and tempo when and if rhythm changes occur.
3. Listen with the objective of identifying each theme well enough to recognize it whenever it is repeated either whole or in part.
4. Take notice of the theme pattern and the way themes are repeated, contrasted, and developed as soon as you are sure of each theme. Observe which themes are given an important share of attention by the composer.
5. Remember that music communication is made through sounds of tone color, harmony and background sound effects in addition to those of rhythm and theme or melody. Be aware of all sounds so that your understanding can reach completion.

Give students the explanation that you feel confident they can learn to hear and understand full content of expression in music without further direction from anyone. For this reason, you are going to introduce each selection with only brief informative remarks about the music. Omit directions to them, and play the music.

Add that you have found the best results to come from hearing the music only once or twice during one class hour, but you will repeat it at their request on other days. When they feel they have gained full understanding of the music, you will give an evaluation exercise so that both they and you can discover how well they have succeeded.

Advise them that there will be questions about rhythm meter and tempo, themes and theme patterns, and relative importance of the themes. They will be asked to write about places in the music which, for them, were especially meaningful and impressive.

A student who has accepted responsibility for hearing the music, and gaining its communication, demands to hear it generally three to six times before he is willing to agree that he fully understands it. This proves to be an important part of his training. He discovers that one cannot hear and understand all of the expression in one hearing. Repetitions are required. In this manner he develops patience and persistence which lead to full understanding of music by the listener.

As the trainee becomes familiar with whole music works, through repetition, he begins to recognize the effect of anticipation on listeners. He notices that certain places in the music are more pleasing and meaningful for him. He realizes that he looks forward to hearing these sounds each time he prepares to listen to the music. The memory or aural image of them comes into his consciousness in recall. He may be working or doing something unrelated to music. The experience of anticipating the sounds, followed by actual realization of what was anticipated, greatly augments a listener's satisfaction with the music. The effect is similar to that of anticipating a return to view of a beloved scene, and the greatly increased pleasure it brings when one sees it again.

Many experienced listeners become so filled with anticipation of the entrance of Movement Four in Beethoven's *Fifth Symphony* that they can scarcely restrain the impulse to applaud or cheer as it begins. For these listeners the aural image of these sounds is so meaningful and emotionally stirring that they look forward to hearing it long before they get to the actual audition.

LISTENING STUDY OF THE FIRST MOVEMENT, "ADAGIO-ALLEGRO-MOLTO" FROM DVORAK'S
NEW WORLD SYMPHONY

Write the name of the music and composer on the blackboard as you introduce it.

Mention that this master composer from Bohemia, now Czechoslovakia, spent several years in our country during the 1890's. The music was inspired by impressions he formed of our country, our people and our culture.

Play the music once on each of several days and repeat it once if requested. Remind listeners to follow the formula which was devised for independent listening. After the fifth hearing and each time after that, ask students if they feel that they hear and understand the whole expression of this music. When they feel that they do, give them an evaluation exercise.

Students are often limited in their powers to express in words what they hear in music. Most of them hear and understand far more than they can describe in words, but we ask them to answer the questions to make certain that they continue to center attention on the music sounds as they are being played.

For variety between repeated hearings have the class sing and hear recordings of several Czech folk songs, Negro spirituals and American Indian folk songs. A recording of Negro spirituals which is favored by students and teachers is *Land of Jordan* by "The Jordanaires."[1] Play "Swing Low Sweet Chariot" and "Let Us Break Bread Together," among others.

When the evaluation exercise is over, papers checked and grades recorded, play the music once more.

Following are some comments about Dvorak's music which are quite typical of listening trainees:

1. The music has two beats in a measure and has a slow-walking tempo in the introduction, "Adagio." When the "Allegro-Molto" begins, the tempo changes abruptly to a rapid, running speed.

---

[1]Capitol Records T 1311, produced by Ken Nelson. Factories, Scranton, Pa. and Los Angeles, California.

2. Theme one has a tone pattern which goes upward aggressively by leaps. It has vigor. There is the long-short, short-long rhythm of the "Scotch snap," heard in this theme.

3. Theme two resembles music of a quaint but joyous folk dance.

4. Theme three resembles the sounds of the "Swing Low" melody.

5. The composer gives greater attention to theme one or the "A" theme. It is repeated whole or in part many times. The "B" theme and "C" theme come in and then "A" theme is developed. The "B" and "C" themes are then repeated several times.

6. Horns play theme one first and immediately afterward the woodwinds play it. They make a contrast in tone color and they seem competitive.

7. Theme two has beautiful harmony. The basses make great surges of tone down in their low range, while the theme is sounding above.

8. Brass tone colors are exciting when they come in with the full orchestra on theme one and when they play the theme development. They add much to the effect of the coda at the end.

9. The tympani sounds add life and zest to the music with their explosive rhythm patterns and rolling drum effects.

10. When the brass takes the melody, the strings play a vigorous tone pattern in the background. When the strings take the melody, the brass plays a tone pattern with harmony in the background.

11. Theme three is very appealing and it grows to be more and more so each time the music is heard.

LISTENING STUDY OF THE THIRD MOVEMENT, " MINUET" FROM BEETHOVEN'S
SYMPHONY NO. 8

Write the name of the music and composer on the blackboard as you introduce it.

Mention that the Eighth Symphony was the next to the last one Beethoven composed. It is neither as dramatic or complex as some of his symphonies, but its meaning and emotional expression have given it significance for each generation of listeners.

Did he write it to be humorous, fun-loving and of lesser importance, or did he write it because he felt that simple uncomplicated meaning best expressed something of special importance?

Play it once and repeat it on the first day. Tell listeners that you will repeat it several times on other days at their request. When they feel assured they have gained a full understanding of the music's communication, they are to make this known and the evaluation exercise will be given.

For variety between repetitions play recordings of Austrian and German folk songs and folk dances, preferably those done in native style and accompaniment.

After papers are checked, and grades recorded, summarize the most discerning answers and read them to the class.

Play the music once more.

Following are some of the comments which are frequently given by trainees about this music of Beethoven's:

1. The rhythm has three beats in a measure. The tempo is in a minuet motion of medium speed.
2. The tempo is a trifle slower when theme two enters.
3. A six-tone rhythm pattern of the two opening measures immediately involves listeners in the motion.
4. Theme one is in the style of a folk dance melody: simple, with a stable, sturdy sound. It is the only theme in the first section of the music, and is heard sometimes whole and sometimes in part.
5. Theme two makes a good contrast with theme one in that it is smooth and graceful.
6. A four-note motive from theme one is repeated in a long series of contrasts, all interesting.
7. The theme pattern reveals a predominance of the "A" theme. "B" theme is introduced and developed in the second section. There is a return to the "A" theme in section three.
8. The French horns play a duet on theme two in a beautiful tone color.
9. The contrast made by horn and clarinet tone colors on theme two is pleasing.

10. Contrasts are made in the rugged bass rhythms in addition to the regular 3/4 rhythm when the accent is on beat one. Another rhythm pattern heard is ♪ ♩ ♩ ♪ . During the playing of theme two the basses play a three-note, short-toned pattern on each beat.
11. Woodwind sounds heard in higher range of the background effects resemble those of a very musical harmonica.

LISTENING STUDY OF BACKGROUND EFFECTS IN VERDI'S "TRIUMPHAL MARCH" FROM *AIDA*, INSTRUMENTAL VERSION

Write the name of the music and composer on the blackboard when you introduce the music.

Students will be familiar with rhythm meter and tempo of the music as well as themes and theme patterns. They learned them in earlier exercises. Modulation of keys will be familiar to them.

In this listening experience they will have an opportunity to become aware of background effects which greatly enhance the musical expression and its meaning.

Two or three repetitions on different days will prove adequate for trainees to complete their hearing understanding of the music's full content.

Tell listeners that you know they are familiar with the rhythm and melody of this music. An evaluation exercise will be given when they feel ready for it. It will have questions on tone color, harmony and background effects.

Following are some of the comments typical of average listening trainees concerning this music:

1. There is a good contrast in the opening fanfare section when the high-range sounds of the brass are heard with the deep full sounds of the basses.
2. Another contrast is evident between the sharp-edged tone texture of trumpets and the more rounded, rich bass tone texture.
3. String tones on the theme of the hymn-like second section make a contrast when they enter with their sustained singing tones following the short detached tones of the brass fanfare.
4. The harmony is beautiful from the strings.

5. Basses play a full velvet-toned rhythm pattern below the strings on section two. They give a constant sense of motion.
6. On the Grand March there is a contrast between smooth trumpet tone and unusually powerful string tones as they alternate on playing the melody.
7. Basses play two different rhythm patterns to accompany the march. On one they give an energetic impetus on each beat. On the other they make a slight push on the long-short note of the measure's second beat. It gives a forward urge to the motion.

When papers are checked and grades recorded, read a summary of the best answers to the class and then have them listen to the music once more.

LISTENING STUDY OF "HUNGARIAN DANCE NO. 5" BY BRAHMS

Write the name of the music and composer on the blackboard as you present it.

Listeners will be aware of the rhythm meter and the rubato tempo of this music from earlier listening experiences. It is probable that they will not have recognized the syncopated accents in the accompanying parts of the background.

The first theme will be familiar to all the listeners; however, most will require repeated hearings in order to identify the other three themes.

Mention to students that the twenty-two "Hungarian Dances" of Brahms were created as piano duets and solos. They became so popular that orchestrations were made later. They have filled a unique place in music literature, and a most favored one.

Ask listeners to hear this music once or twice on different days until they feel they fully understand it. Tell them you will ask in the evaluation exercises for the rhythm meter, tempo and background rhythm patterns, the themes and their patterns. You will want comments on the special impressions that endure in their aural images of the music's sounds.

Following are some observations typical of average trainees concerning this music of Brahms:

1. There are two beats in a measure of rhythm. The tempo is rapid and vigorous. It changes into rubato tempo frequently.
2. There is a syncopated accent in the rhythm of the lower range sounds.
3. The music includes four different themes. The "A" and "B" themes are given greater attention. The "D" theme gets less and the "C" theme least of all.
4. The harmonies stir imagination and may be described as hauntingly beautiful for they linger in mind and return often in memory.
5. Rubato tempo makes a feeling of suspense in places.
6. String tone colors are one of the music's most pleasing expressions.
7. There are flashes of tingling sound from the triangle which add gaiety and excitement to the music expression.

CHAPTER FOURTEEN

Extending Experiences to Create
Listener Independence

Music selections presented in this chapter offer a wide variety in styles of expression. Each composer reflects something of the expression of his people. He also has characteristic expressions of his own which set him apart from the others.

Students will gain a good measure of understanding by hearing a selection about six times. They will add to that understanding each time they hear the music for some time after their training period ends. Many of them discover this to be true and they comment on it when you encounter them at concerts or when they visit school.

LISTENING STUDY OF SMETANA'S
"THE MOLDAU"

Write the name of the music and composer on the blackboard as you introduce it.

Students will be familiar with the themes and motives of this music from former exercises. The hunting scene theme will be the only exception.

Tell listeners that you will play the music once or twice on one day. You will repeat it at their request on other days. When they feel that their understanding is adequate, you will give an evaluation exercise.

Add that you will ask for meter and tempo identification and any changes made in them throughout the music. You will ask for them to recognize theme pattern and to describe parts of the music which were especially meaningful and impressive to them.

Mention that Smetana, the composer, wrote a cycle of symphonic poems to pay tribute to his country, at that time named Bohemia, but now known as Czechoslovakia. "The Moldau" is the second one in the cycle.

The music is named for the longest river in the country. This is program music, depicting scenes from life along the river as it flows through the land. The scenes which receive special attention are:

● Two tiny streams flowing down through the forest-covered mountain where they meet and join to form the start of a river.
● The breadth and grandeur of the river.
● A hunting scene.
● A peasant wedding scene.
● Moonlight on the river where an imaginary nymph dance is taking place.
● River flowing over St. John's Rapids.
● The old castle and fortress of Vysehrad, where dramatic scenes of history have occurred.

When papers from the evaluation exercises have been checked, and grades recorded, read a summary of the better comments on the music to the class. Play the music again.

Following are some listener comments which are typical:

1. The rhythm meter begins with six beats in a measure. The tempo is rapid.
2. On the peasant dance the meter changes to two beats in a measure. The motion and tempo slow down to that of a brisk walk.
3. On the moonlight theme, the rhythm meter changes once more just where the key changes. There are four

beats in a measure. The tempo resembles a moderate walking speed.

4. When the moonlight theme section ends, the rhythm meter returns to six beats in a measure and rapid tempo. The key changes to major on the river theme in place of minor as was heard in the first part of the music.

5. There are two separate tone patterns sounding in the opening part of the music. They are in flute and clarinet tone colors. The viola comes in for a short time.

6. The music includes four themes. A chant-like motive is repeated in the final section.

7. The first theme is called "River Theme." Its sounds express a feeling that the river passes in a joyous, sweeping motion. The composer repeats this theme much more than the others. It is heard several times in the same minor key and then repeated several times at a lower range. Violins and oboes introduce it, and then flute and bassoon tone colors are heard joining in.

   The volume and depth of the river are represented by a build-up in tone by adding more instruments, by crescendos, and by increasing fullness of bass tones.

8. The hunting scene has a rhythm pattern played in two-part harmony on the horns. They imitate the sounds of galloping horses' hooves. Above them the trumpets play a four-toned pattern of notes which go up similar to a flash of fireworks. The brasses are heard on the theme which is in bugle call style. The pattern played by horns is echoed by other instruments of the orchestra. The horns have a distant sound.

9. In the peasant dance the harmony is beautiful. The theme is made out of a combination of short staccato tones and smooth singing sounds.

10. The tympani accents the dance rhythm with a soft, rounded tone. The triangle alternates with the tympani in making the accent.

11. Moonlight theme is as light and flowing as part of the peasant dance is sturdy and bouncing.

12. In the section depicting St. John's Rapids, the river theme is heard in short fragments from various instru-

ments. The sounds seem to be whirled around in a great tumult.

13. In the final scene the strings make a swell in volume on the river theme.
14. All the instruments except the strings play the chant-style motive in great, dramatic chords.

LISTENING STUDY OF THE SECOND MOVEMENT OF BEETHOVEN'S *SYMPHONY NO. 6*

Write the name of the music and composer on the blackboard as you introduce it.

Listeners will be familiar with the motive which is heard accompanying at the beginning of the music and continuing two-thirds of the way through the selection. It is known as the "Brook Motive." They will remember themes one and three which were heard in exercises from chapters 5 and 6. Theme two will be the only one left for them to identify and learn to remember.

Trainees will find this music more complex and contrasts more subtle than in most other program music. Obvious and dramatic contrasts are not to be found here. It brings to listeners a most enjoyable experience with string and woodwind tone colors. Meaning and pleasure increase for the audience with each additional hearing.

Explain to students that Beethoven truly appreciated the beauty of nature in the great outdoors. He named the symphony "Pastoral" and the second movement "By the Brook."

Mention that the music differs from customary program music in that it does not tell a story, create a mood, or picture events in sound. It recreates feelings, through musical expression, which came to the composer when he gained inspiration to write the music. It becomes obvious to students early in our listening study that his feelings and perceptions were deep and profound.

Tell students you will play the music and repeat it at their request until they feel confident of understanding its communication. When they agree that they are ready you will give an evaluation exercise to find how well they have understood.

Tell them you will ask about rhythm meter, tempo, themes and theme pattern. You will ask for their descriptions of places in the music which left an especially deep impression and aural image of the music.

A recording of this music which has remained a long time favorite is Beethoven's "Pastoral" Symphony, Fritz Reiner and Chicago Symphony.[1]

When the papers from the evaluation exercise have been checked, and grades recorded, read the class a summary of the better comments and then play the music once more.

Following are some fairly typical comments made by trainees upon hearing and learning to understand this music of Beethoven:

1. The rhythm meter has 12 beats in a measure. The tempo is similar to a lively dance step done in groups of three steps, on the toes.

2. There is a motive or tone pattern from the low strings beginning at the first of the music and continuing through most of the movement. It stimulates a sense of constant motion.

3. Theme one enters at the end of the first measure in high-range violin tone color. It is beautiful and impressive in these ways:

   Color and texture of tone.

   Meaning or expression of theme.

   It is the only sound one hears beside the rhythm and tone pattern of the low strings, with which it contrasts. The effect it makes etches the theme on memory and causes it to be recalled often.

4. Theme two immediately follows the second playing of theme one. It enters in string tone color, beginning with a long sustained tone. Then it moves in a light dance step pattern—down and up first, and then up and down. It is repeated once.

5. Theme three enters in low-range tones. Its motion is suggestive of a smooth, graceful group dance. The feeling of motion is pleasing.

6. The final section, coda, has imitation bird calls which make appealing tone patterns in contrasting tone colors and textures.

7. Theme one is given much greater attention by the composer.

---

[1] RCA Red Seal Dynagroove; L.S.C.–2614 or Mono L M 2614.

8. In the two opening themes, there is a pleasing contrast in tone color and texture between string and woodwinds.
9. When theme three enters the first time, violas and bassoons play it. Sometimes they alternate. When they do there is a tone texture contrast.
10. There is a passage shortly after theme three enters, followed by theme one, where flute plays marvelous embellishments. The low strings are playing sustained tones in harmony at that same time. The violin plays a tone pattern in the background. It is a delightful section.
11. When the final third of the music begins, theme three returns. Woodwinds and strings alternate on the melody. The basses play a tone and rhythm pattern down below by plucking the strings.

LISTENING STUDY OF "DANSE BOHEME" FROM *CARMEN SUITE* BY BIZET

Write the name of the composer and the music on the blackboard before you introduce it.

Explain that the music is taken from a colorful and dramatic scene in the opera. It is built around a group scene of gypsy dancers, dressed in bright colors and carrying castanets and tambourines which they play while dancing.

Mention that gypsy dances customarily are created with zestful leaps, rapid whirling and sudden tempo changes. The dancers fascinate observers because they appear to be free of all care and seem to possess the power and agility of super beings.

Gypsies choose bright contrasts of color in their apparel. They wear numerous bracelets, necklaces, rings, and earrings. The same taste is demonstrated in their music with ornamentation and embellishments. They seem to have fascinated Bizet as they do others, for he included their characteristics in his music.

You may want to review the folk song, "Spanish Gypsies," by having the class sing it. It relates well to the Bizet music.

Play the music once on each of several days and repeat it if requested. When students feel that they hear and understand the full expression of the music, give an evaluation exercise.

Advise students you will ask for meter measure and tempo. You will expect recognition of themes and their pattern of succession.

You will want descriptions of the places in the music which impressed them and were most meaningful to them.

After papers are checked and grades recorded, read a summary of the better comments to the class. Play the music again.

Following are some comments typical of trainees concerning Bizet's music:

1. The music has three beats in a measure. The tempo is comparable to that of a brisk walking step.

2. Theme one is an animated tune played by flutes, in harmony, when it enters. It is repeated many times. The pitch is lowered each time, which adds variety. This may be intended to represent the entrance of an added dancer each time.

3. Theme two moves in a pattern which ascends over wide skips. It moves with great energy as though the dancers might be running to effect high leaps.

4. Rhythm patterns of both theme three and theme one suggest three long leaps followed by whirling motions.

5. Themes one and three receive most of the composer's attention.

6. In the opening section, where theme one is repeated about ten times, there is high excitement because the motion continues with such spirit. The listener identifies with it spontaneously.

7. An expressive effect which returns often in memory comes when the tambourines are shaken in a long crescendo. It terminates in a loud clash by the percussion instruments.

8. Bizet creates overwhelming excitement in the final section of the music when themes three and one are repeated over and over with increasing tempo. In the background we hear the lower-toned instruments, and the percussions playing an accent after each beat in syncopated style. The volume grows with the tempo increase. It moves to a terrific climax.

9. Tone color and texture contrasts are made between the strings and woodwinds. The brass comes in for short bright flashes. Percussion sounds contribute much to the music's expression.

10. Triangles, castanets and tambourines add special excitement and beauty to the rhythm. They stir the imagination and create a sense of life and added motion.

LISTENING STUDY OF "OVERTURE"
TO THE OPERA *MIGNON*
BY AMBROISE THOMAS

Write the name of the music and composer on the blackboard as you introduce it.

The numerous themes included in this music will, in all probability, be new and strange to trainees. Each theme is impressive and meaningful. Students have little trouble in learning them with a few repetitions, with the exception of theme four. It is elusive and intricate.

Remind listeners that an overture customarily includes themes from leading melodies of the opera it precedes.

The 1A and 1B themes are heard only at the first of the music. They are both from this opera's most beloved song, "Connais-tu le pays?" (Know'st thou the land?)

Teach the class to sing an English translation of this exceptionally appealing melody.

Play the overture once on each of several days and repeat it if requested. Tell students you will review it on other days until they feel sure they fully understand the music. At that time, an evaluation exercise will be given.

When papers have been checked and grades recorded, read a summary of the better comments to the class and then play the music again.

Following are some typical comments of trainees concerning this music:

1. The introduction of this music is made up of cadenzas and ad-lib passages. It is difficult to recognize an established meter. The meter of theme one has six beats in a measure. The tempo is similar to a rapid walking speed.
2. The several beautiful cadenzas in the opening measures start the music off in an atmosphere of wonder and magic. The tone colors are appealing and beautifully contrasted.
3. As theme two enters, the meter changes to three beats

in a measure. Its tempo is slightly faster than that of a medium walking speed.

4. Themes 1A and 1B charm the listener so much that he keeps hoping all through the music to hear them repeated.

5. Themes two and three are each in the style of a dance, the polonaise.

6. Theme four is very difficult to identify. Its melody and rhythm are both unusual and complex. It is worth the required struggle to learn it because it gets more appealing each time the music is heard.

7. The composer gives his greatest attention to themes two and three.

8. An unforgettable part of this music is the harp cadenza which comes in the introduction. The tone color sounds so warm and resonant it seems to extend and fill all of space. Its sounds are heard all alone. Other strings finally join in and then a background tone pattern comes from the oboe or English horn. It makes harmony with the harp tones.

9. The entrance of beautiful theme one in horn tone color makes a profound impression on listeners. The strings play sustained harmony tones with the horns.

10. The 1B theme comes in soaring violin tones of great beauty. The harp is heard strumming in the background. There are rich singing tones from the basses. Horns play sustained tones in the background which harmonize with the melody. The sounds are wonderful.

11. There is a lively and pleasing contrast where the woodwinds and strings alternate with each other repeatedly on theme three. The low strings and horns make a boisterous "wump-wump" down below the other sounds at the same time.

CHAPTER FIFTEEN

Testing Trainees' Listening Skills on Mozart's Music, and Others

The instructor will have established habitual student use of the formula for listening study of music works new to the listener.

As we present music from a major work of Mozart, we take on a daring challenge. This composer's musical expression has restraint, subtlety and complexity which call for advanced skill in the listener. Superficial understanding of Mozart's music has sometimes created for it an image of joyous, pleasant-sounding music which lacks depth or perception which are of significance.

The first, and one of the most important assets our trainees have to protect them from the fallacy of such a view, is that they will have learned to listen at the composer's tempo. This keeps them abreast of the sounds as they are initiated. In addition trainees respond with rapid reaction awareness to the sounds of each music element. The sounds are not out and away before our listeners hear them.

Students will gain a substantial beginning to understanding whole communication of this music during our class presentations. They will complete this objective, with extended pleasure, as they hear repetitions of the music over the coming years. Interest awakened through class study will motivate them to pursue the objective of achieving complete understanding. We can be assured of this because we know that listeners never outgrow Mozart's music. The reverse is true. The more a student understands Mozart's music, the more he is inclined to seek further experience with it.

LISTENING STUDY OF THE FIRST MOVEMENT, "ADAGIO: ALLEGRO" FROM MOZART'S *SYMPHONY NO. 39*

Write the name of the music and the composer on the blackboard as you introduce it.

Theme one of this allegro movement will be familiar to listeners from exercises in Chapters 6 and 7 on identification of motion and tempo.

Explain that this symphony was one of the final three written by Mozart. It has been acclaimed as one of his finest works.

Mention to the students that you will play the music once on each of several days and repeat it upon their request until they agree that they understand its communication. When they do, you will give an evaluation exercise.

Add that you will ask about rhythm meter and tempo which are heard at the beginning of the music. You will want recognition of any changes in them through the entire movement. You will ask about themes and their patterns. Request descriptions of places in the music which are especially meaningful or impressive to the listener.

Warn students that this composer customarily employs restraint in emotional expression and in contrasts. He does not make his expression glaringly obvious. This is not because he wishes to be elusive, but because he assumes listeners will be skillful in hearing all facets of his expression without having them forced on the sense of hearing. Owing to his own musical genius and sensitivity to sound, he expected more sensitivity in his listeners than the average person possesses until his listening skills have been developed. When they have, Mozart's music requires full use of that skill at all times.

When papers from the evaluation exercise have been checked

and grades recorded, read a summary of the better comments to the class and play the music once more.

Following are some typical listener comments about this music of Mozart:

1. The adagio introduction meter has four beats in a measure. The tempo is similar to the speed of an easy walking step.

2. When the "Allegro" enters, the meter changes to three beats in a measure and the tempo changes to one suitable for an easy running speed.

3. The introduction begins in impressive chords of great majesty. They come in a rhythm pattern of ♩ ♩. ♪|♩. . Alternating with it scale passages are heard descending over more than an octave.

4. The chords come in woodwind and bass tone colors, but the descending scale passages are done with smooth grace by the strings.

5. Theme one enters as the allegro tempo begins. It is played the first time by higher strings, and the second time by lower-voiced strings. Woodwinds echo the theme above the lower strings during the second playing of the theme.

6. Theme two has a more active rhythm pattern than theme one. This makes a contrast while distinguishing one from the other. Woodwinds are heard alternating at intervals.

7. Theme three moves with smoother grace than either of the other themes.

8. Theme one receives slightly more attention from the composer.

9. The harmonies and the chromatic sounds of the introduction are disturbing. They introduce a suggestion of menace or tragedy.

10. When theme one enters the first time, it follows the hesitant, chromatic tones which close the introduction. The happy melody of theme one makes a delightful contrast for listeners. Its motion seems so free of effort.

11. In the connecting passages and the development sounds of the themes there is an energetic, bustling rhythm

motion that contrasts with the serenity and grace of the themes motion.

12. The patterns of descending scale tones from the introduction are heard in connecting passages of the "Allegro."

Trainees' expressions of deep satisfaction and pleasure from study of Mozart's music have developed an instructors' consensus that every student should be given a good chance to understand his music. Their comments indicate that they consider the listening study of Mozart an outstanding privilege and experience.

LISTENING STUDY OF THE THIRD MOVEMENT, "MINUETTO ALLEGRETTO" FROM MOZART'S *SYMPHONY NO. 39*

Write the name of the music and the composer on the blackboard when you introduce it.

Students will be familiar with the themes from having heard them in exercises from Chapters 7 and 10 on rhythm motion, tempo and harmony.

Explain to the class that this minuetto is said to be known around the world. Its two themes are truly appealing and they make a pleasing contrast. There is something of the warm good fellowship and energetic motion of Austrian folk dances in the sounds of theme one. The second theme has all the grace of a waltz.

Tell the class you will play the music once on each of several days and repeat it at their request. When they agree that they understand all of the music, you will give an evaluation exercise.

Add that you will ask about tempo, rhythm meter motion, themes and theme pattern. You will want descriptions of places in the music which are particularly impressive and meaningful to the listeners.

When papers from the evaluation exercise have been checked and grades recorded, read a summary of the better comments to the class and play the music once more.

Following are some typical student comments about this music of Mozart:

1. The meter has three beats in a measure. The tempo and motion bustle, and are vigorous for a minuet. It moves

with a speed similar to medium running steps. It has the sound of a gay and zestful waltz.

2. The rhythm of theme one is expressive of a strong and active motion. At first the tone pattern of the theme skips up and down and then it climbs up. It is heard over and over in the first part of the movement.

3. Theme two is even more appealing than theme one. It drifts often through memory. Its motion is smoother than that of theme one. There is suggestion of a group gaily moving around in unison. A listener cannot escape identification with its motion. He gets caught up by it.

4. Theme one gets greater attention from the composer.

5. String tone color is heard on theme one much of the time. Bow strokes are brisk and rowdy.

6. Theme two is played by clarinets. They make tone color and texture contrasts with the string tones which were heard on theme one. There is a violin tone passage sounding here and there between repetitions of theme two. The violin tone is very mellow on this passage.

7. While theme two is sounding there is a rhythm pattern in the background. It has two notes to a beat which add a continuous feeling of motion.

8. In the background of theme one there is a chromatic, descending passage by viola or 'cello which makes a slight feeling of melancholy.

9. During the first half of theme one there is a brisk bowing on the beat by the lower-toned instruments.

Teacher A made a practice of not telling students the name of the music or composer in either of the two presentations of Mozart until after the evaluation exercises were completed. The students were intrigued with the mystery and very attentive. They had no opportunity to go to the library and read an analysis of this music which could influence their answers in the evaluation exercises.

Teacher B had a customary procedure, when giving the evaluation exercise, of stopping the music here and there and requesting trainees to write which theme or which tone color they were hearing when the music stopped. He felt that this helped to keep them constantly alert and aware to the degree required for understanding Mozart.

LISTENING STUDY OF "SUNRISE" FROM *THE GRAND CANYON SUITE* BY FERDE GROFÉ

Write the name of the music and the composer on the blackboard as you introduce it.

The more famous selection from this suite is probably "On the Trail." The other selections are fully as interesting. The opening one which we are presenting has become a great favorite with listeners.

Mention to students that Grofé, an American composer, has long been famous for his program music. He describes scenes of our country and his feelings about them in tone paintings as Smetana did about his country in "The Moldau." Grofé has composed suites about the Mississippi River, the Hudson River and others. Music of the *Grand Canyon Suite* has become most widely known.

A rugged beauty and awesome effect of the Grand Canyon have been the inspiration for many creative works. The spectacle and the grandeur of the canyon overwhelm and stagger the senses of its viewers. It is not uncommon for people to weep as they receive the first view of this natural wonder.

Explain that the music they are to hear is a tonal expression of the gradual change in view, beginning with the semi-darkness of early morning to the time when the sunshine reveals the vivid colors of the canyon in a light of dazzling brightness.

Most students will be familiar with Grieg's beautiful "Morning" from *Peer Gynt Suite.* It is helpful to compare the two selections after the class hears Grofé's music. Grieg's music reflects a peaceful stillness of morning. A listener feels the quiet newness of the day. The mood remains tranquil throughout. Grofé's music suggests an increasingly spectacular event which develops feelings of excitement and awe of tremendous proportions. It increases in volume and bright tone textures as it moves into a great and prolonged burst of sound.

Tell the students that you will play the music once on each of several days and repeat it on others at their request. When they feel satisfied that they understand the music, you will give an evaluation exercise.

Add that you will want to know about meter measure, tempos,

theme identification and pattern. You will ask them to describe places in the music which were especially meaningful and impressive to listeners.

Following are some trainee comments which are typical concerning this music of Grofé:

1. The meter has six beats in a measure. The tempo is at the speed of light running steps.
2. Theme one makes a western style, carefree expression, with tones undulating and then gradually descending. It is played first in flute tone color, then on English horn. Later these two instruments alternate on playing the theme. Theme one receives slightly more composer attention than theme two.
3. Theme two is first heard in string tone color. The tone pattern decends by skips and then ascends scalewise. It receives developmental treatment.
4. The first sound in the music is a soft roll from the tympani. In the next second the higher strings are heard in sustained dissonant tones. The sounds are lonely and eerie. A feeling of mystery comes from the expression.
5. When the piccolo enters on the bird call-like sounds, the mood changes.
6. While theme one is being played on the flutes, at first, the horns echo the theme sounds in the background. When the flutes and English horn alternate on theme one, the harp is heard in beautiful tone color playing in the background. Later, tones of the celesta join in the sound.
7. Theme two expresses a pleasant feeling of well-being and contentment which drifts through memory after it ceases to be heard. The harp is played in background sounds. The low strings echo theme two as it is played by the violins.
8. The whole orchestra gradually builds up volume of tone as the day brightens and development of theme two continues.
9. High strings come back on theme one and the music swells in a gigantic build-up as all the splendor of sunlight on the red and gold colors of the canyon appear.

The basses increase volume. The whole orchestra rises in a crescendo. The tympani beats a pattern in repeated accents. It is wonderfully exciting.

10. This music has an unusual effect on listeners. You can play it when you feel out of sorts with everyone and everything and by the time it is completed, you have forgotten why you felt that way. All is right in your world once more.

LISTENING STUDY OF THE THIRD MOVEMENT, "PRESTO" FROM BEETHOVEN'S *SYMPHONY NO. 7*

Write the name of the music and the composer on the blackboard as you present it.

Mention to listeners that this Third Movement of Beethoven is marked "Presto" on the score, but generally referred to as "Scherzo" because it is in that style. It is placed where a scherzo is customarily found in the symphony pattern.

Add that the word "scherzo" is Italian and means "joke." It makes a humorous or playful impression. There is one unusual trait about this one. The trio part is repeated in a second place in the movement. The design or form is thus changed to A B A B A.

Tell the trainees you will play the music once on each of several days and will repeat it at their request. When they agree that they understand the music in full, you will give an evaluation exercise.

Add that you will want to know what meter measures and tempo were heard. You will want identification of themes and their patterns. You will ask for descriptions of places in the music which were most impressive and meaningful to listeners.

Following are some listener comments which are typical concerning this music of Beethoven:

1. The meter has three beats in a measure. The tempo on theme one is rapid. It could be described as a scurrying motion except that it has greater vigor. On themes two and three the tempo is similar to the rhythm of a lively waltz. The two tempos contrast sharply.

2. Theme one has a tone pattern which descends stepwise,

leaps back up to a high pitch and then descends once more. Great zest and energy are expressed in the feeling of its motion. When this theme is heard first, it is in clarinet tone colors.

3. The melody of theme two resembles a folk hymn in style. It is heard in a changed key and comes in two-part harmony.

4. Theme three has a range of only five tones which are long sustained. It has a soothing effect through its flow of tone.

5. Theme one is heard in sections one, three and five of the music. Themes two and three are heard in sections two and four. The themes are developed in each of these sections.

6. "Scherzo" suggests a mood of joking or playfulness and Beethoven starts the music true to style. The sounds enter at such speed and zest that the listener must "leap" to attention if he is to identify with the motion. This is true every time theme one re-enters after the slower tempos of themes two and three.

7. The tympani sounds generate excitement and contrast all through the movement.

8. When theme two begins the second section it is heard in horn tone color. After it is heard twice, the horns repeat the motive from the first half of the theme. A flute plays the motive in a higher range at the same time, while strings sustain harmony tones in the background. After a little, the woodwinds join in playing theme three in higher range. The sounds from this section make a deep impression on the listener. They return often in memory.

9. A very exciting place comes in the music where the full orchestra plays theme two and the brasses are heard in a bright, sustained tone which comes through like a shaft of brilliant sunlight.

10. There are many pleasing contrasts in tone color as theme one is heard from various instruments in development sections.

An Afterword from the Author

Instructors customarily evaluate the accomplishments of each listening skill training group as their work nears completion. These evaluations express pride and satisfaction in the substantial evidence of student progress.

Teachers place high value on provisions in the training exercises for preventing two destructive habits from emerging. These two are day dreaming and preoccupation in thought at the time active listening is required. Activities keep students involved in a manner which leaves no opportunity for either obstacle to arise.

Highest praise and a rating of "outstanding innovation" repeatedly go to two other provisions in the exercises. One is the provision for developing identification, through hearing, of the sounds of each music element. The other is that of development of individual reaction awareness of the sounds of each music element.

By the close of their training period, students are sufficiently skillful to continue study of music literature independently. These listeners are delightful to work with in advanced music literature classes.

For independent study progress, listeners require excellent recordings with related equipment. They need a place in which to listen where they will be free from interruptions or distractions. The place should be one where they will not be forcing the sounds

203

of their music on others who cannot understand it and who therefore object to the sounds.

In communities where professional live concerts or radio broadcasts of music literature are not available, some experiments have been made in giving concerts with recordings. They were created and designed for ex-trainees and other capable listeners in the community.

They have been well received. They were especially appreciated by those who did not have a suitable place at home to progress with their listening studies. The concerts were from forty-five minutes to an hour in length. The programs of music selections were announced well in advance of the concert time. Some programs were sponsored by schools, others by community organizations. One was a joint project of college and adult education groups.

Evidence developed from evaluation of music listening skill trainee responses indicates that understanding of the communication in music literature is within the capabilities of all individuals who have an opportunity to develop their listening skills.

INDEX

A

"Absolute Music," 164
Accents, in rhythm, 87-93
Accompaniment, 41
Active and rest tones, 52-55
Afro-American Symphony, 92
"Afternoon of a Faun," Debussy,
   126, 137, 145
Aida, 24, 69, 76, 82, 149, 179-180
"America," 39
"American Salute," 128
"America, the Beautiful," 49
"Among the Olive Trees," 33, 36
"Andalusia," 33
Anthems, 39
Appalachian Spring, 83, 168
"Auld Lang Syne," 75
Aural image, 59

B

Bach's "Jesu, Joy of Man's Desiring,"
   64-65, 130, 136
Background, 93-95
Baritone, 154-156
Bass, 156-157
Basses, 42
Bassoon, 127-129
"Battle Hymn of the Republic," 68
Beethoven:
   Eroica Symphony, 67, 96
   Fifth Symphony, 49, 67, 78, 102,
      106-107, 121, 134-135,
      138, 175
   "Pastoral" Symphony, 187
   Symphony No. 6, 77, 78, 84, 91-92,
      96, 151, 186-188
   Symphony No. 7,
      200-201
   Symphony No. 8, 128-129, 169,
      177-179
   Symphony No. 9, 78-79, 95, 131
Binary form, 165, 166
Bizet (*see Carmen Suite*)
"Bolero," 51
Brahms:
   C Minor Symphony, 51
   "Hungarian Dance No. 5," 122, 180-181
   "Hungarian Dance No. 6," 76-77,
      132
   "Lullaby," 110
   Symphony No. 1, 143
Brass instrument family, 23, 40
Britten, 51, 117-118
"Brother John," 50
"Brown Eyes," 33

C

Cadence, hearing identification, 68-69
"Capriccio Italien," 33, 41, 42, 60-64,
   70, 93, 94, 105, 121, 136, 142
"Cara Nina," 33
Carmen Suite, 33, 36, 41, 44, 55-56, 69,
   74, 82, 91, 94, 95, 120, 125, 126,
   133, 137, 141, 188-190
Carnival of the Animals, 79
"Cattle Blues," 167-168
Chabrier, 51

Chavez, "Toccata for Percussion," 141
"Cheyenne War Dance," 56, 90
Chopin, "Etude in A^b," 135
Chromatic scale tones, 73, 74, 75
"Clair de Lune," 142-143
Clarinets, tone color, 111-113
Coloratura soprano, 156-158
"Come Sailing With Me," 31
"Comin' Through the Rye," 55
Complete cadence, 68

Composer:
   communication with listener, 59-71
   hearing identification of cadence,
      68-69
   introducing French horn, 66-68
   musical idom, 32-34
   themes, employing dash pattern,
      60-66
   two or more music elements, 69-71
"Concerto For Trumpet," 45
Consonance:
   balanced with dissonance, 124
   chord of resolution, 124
   dull, tiresome music, 124
   examples, 123

   excessive use, 124
   following dissonance, 123, 124
   restful effect, 124
Contra-bassoon, 127-129
Contralto, 158-159

Contrasts:
   consonance, 123-125
   dissonance, 123-125
   flute tone colors, 125-126
   form, 164, 165
   motion in uneven rhythm, 119-122
   piccolo tone color, 125-126
   string tone colors, 116-119
"Coronation Marche-Le Prophete," 113

Correcting papers, 39
Countries, rhythm patterns, 55-58
Cymbals, 36, 37
"Czardas," 120